Powerful Synergy

Stories of Entrepreneurship and Motherhood Strengthening Each Other

Featuring Author Marta Sauret Greca

Stories Collected by Cori Wamsley

Aurora Corialis Publishing

Pittsburgh, PA

POWERFUL SYNERGY: STORIES OF ENTREPRENEURSHIP AND MOTHERHOOD STRENGTHENING EACH OTHER

Copyright © 2024 by Marta Sauret Greca

All rights reserved. No part of this book may be used, reproduced, stored in a retrieval system, or transmitted by any means—electronic, mechanical, photocopy, microfilm, recording, or otherwise—without written permission from the publisher, except in the case of brief quotations embodied in critical articles or reviews. For more information, address: cori@auroracorialispublishing.com.

All external reference links utilized in this book have been validated to the best of our ability and are current as of publication.

The publisher and the authors make no guarantees concerning the level of success you may experience by following the advice and strategies contained in this book, and the reader accepts the risk that results will differ for each individual.

Neither the authors nor the publisher assumes any responsibility for errors, omissions, or contrary interpretations of the subject matter herein. Any perceived slight of an individual or organization is purely unintentional.

To ensure privacy and confidentiality, some names or other identifying characteristics of the persons included in this book may have been changed. All the personal examples of the authors' own life and experiences have not been altered.

Printed in the United States of America

Edited by: Allison Hrip, Aurora Corialis Publishing

Cover Design: Karen Captline, BetterBe Creative

Paperback ISBN: 978-1-958481-34-9

Ebook ISBN: 978-1-958481-35-6

Praise for Powerful Synergy

"These entrepreneur moms share impactful and heartfelt stories that genuinely capture the complexities of balancing a dream job and motherhood. Their honest reflection on feeling pulled in multiple directions and striving for 'a life you love' offer invaluable insights that resonate. Their tenacity and positivity shine through, showing how managing your mindset and belief in yourself can lead to true fulfillment and success. An inspiring read for anyone struggling to harmonize entrepreneurial or career ambitions with the joys of parenthood!"

~ Amy Hooper Hanna
Leadership Coach
Author of *For She Who Grieves: Practical Wisdom for Living Hope*

"What an inspiring read! Leaving the corporate world to start your own business is no small feat, I know. But these powerhouse moms prove that the leap is worth it! This book is a testament to how motherhood can fuel entrepreneurial spirit; we all have it in us! They are turning bedtime stories into boardroom strategies. Get ready to laugh, cheer, and be utterly convinced that the joy of running your own show beats corporate cubicles any day. Here's to the unstoppable, sassy mom bosses!"

- Windie King
Store Manager, The Container Store Pittsburgh

"As a woman who started her own business after raising two children and becoming an 'empty nester,' I have always been amazed and inspired by women who balance little ones and their own business. I now have written proof as to why!

"The anthology *Powerful Synergy: Stories of Entrepreneurship and Motherhood Strengthening Each Other* is a compelling collection that dives into the personal and professional journeys of twelve women. Through their stories, readers gain insights into the diverse challenges and triumphs these women have faced, highlighting the intersection of family influence and business success.

"I highly recommend this book as a great resource to any woman in business, but especially for those moms who might need an extra 'You can do it!' every now and again."

~ Kelli A. Komondor
CEO & Visibility Strategist
K2 Creative Strategies

"This is the book to read if you're considering business ownership, as it's written by a group of mothers who have conquered both motherhood and the business world. The gift of time and availability are found in the many instances required in motherhood: whether that's a school PTA meeting or a NICU stay. Entrepreneurship is the way we collectively are able to cater to our children."

~Charissa Lauren
Publicist and Owner of Charissa Lauren Collective and FAME by CL
Co-Author of *Mom Magic*

"I can honestly say that this is the book you need if you are juggling the worlds of being both a mother and entrepreneur! The women whose stories are shared in *Powerful Synergy: Stories of Entrepreneurship and Motherhood Strengthening Each Other* are amazing business owners with huge hearts for their families. While reading this book, you will uncover secrets of success that were written by women, some of whom wrote their chapter while breastfeeding, balancing business and home budgets, and/or while finally taking some well-deserved *me time* to reflect on their life's work!"

~Dr. Shellie Hipsky
Founder and Executive Director of The Global Sisterhood Nonprofit
International Speaker and Coach
Author of *From Ball Gowns to Yoga Pants* and Other Inspiring Books

"*Powerful Synergy: Stories of Entrepreneurship and Motherhood Strengthening Each Other* is a powerful testament to the resilience and determination of women who balance the demands of motherhood and entrepreneurship. Each chapter offers a peek into the lives of remarkable women who, despite setbacks and heartbreaks, found the courage to prioritize themselves—not just as mothers, but as individuals with dreams, ambitions, and a deep sense of self-worth. Their stories are filled with catalyst moments where they had to make tough choices to ensure they could be the best version of themselves, both as entrepreneurs and as mothers.

"They remind us that choosing oneself is not a selfish act, but rather an essential step in becoming the kind of mother and leader that their families, businesses, and communities need. Their stories will resonate deeply with any woman who has ever had to balance the demands of motherhood with the pursuit of her dreams."

~ Tracy Montarti
Photographer, Educator, and Midlife Renaissance™ Strategist, guiding Midlife Women to discover Clarity, Purpose, and Legacy in Their Second Act

Table of Contents

Introduction i
    Cori Wamsley.. i
Foreword v
    Marta Sauret Greca v
Maverick Moments 1
    Marta Sauret Greca 1
Hustling for Survival 15
    Tanya Bashor 15
Wherever You Go 23
    Samantha Bauer 23
Taking Back Your POWER While Balancing Babies and Business 31
    Emma Ferrick 31
Embracing What You Never Saw Coming 41
    Ashley Fina 41
From Special Education Teacher to Homeschool Mompreneur 49
    Christine Furman 49
I Do. I Did. I'm Done! Surviving to Thriving in Motherhood, Divorce, and Entrepreneurship 57
    Melissa Ghelarducci Hancock 57
Recovering from American Dream Burnout 67
    Diane Greco Allen 67
My Journey to Creating Freedom and Being Present in Business and Family 77

Priscilla Green 77

Loving Mondays 85
Erika Maddamma 85

A Season for Every Purpose 93
Theresa Ream 93

My Recipe for Lemonade 103
Kara Taylor 103

Continuing the Connection 111
A Note from the Authors 111

About The Global Sisterhood 113

Introduction

Cori Wamsley

Every mother has a story about how it seemed like you were experiencing the end of the world, but then you got a nudge from God, Universe, Source that put you on the path you were meant to be on. It's funny how that tweak then lets us soar as business owners!

Women are so dynamic, though, that we often look at our challenges as little blips that interrupt our flow. We get through them. And then we keep going without looking back because, honestly, we are programmed to keep up that sprint. This book celebrates how resilient mothers are and how we strive for more in our own lives *because* we are mothers. Our children help us push through, rise above, and rock on!

The stories of perseverance during difficult moments shared in this book showcase women in times when they thought their world—personal, professional, or both—was crashing down around them, but truly, it was the beginning to their purpose being active in their lives, their calling ignited. In that difficult moment, being a mom was a driver and inspiration for these women.

Their families were their inspiration.

There's this myth that when you become a mother, your career, self-care—basically life as you knew it—is over. But the mothers in this book *know* that the genuine Divine truth is that having children can infuse success into your life. Their stories of perseverance in motherhood and business go beyond just discussing the systems and processes that helped them reach the big goals in their lives: they also inspire us with what kept them striving for more!

Powerful Synergy

As the mother of two "tweenage" daughters who have been keeping me on my toes for just over a decade while I built my business, I relate to so much in these stories. I actually started my freelance writing business right after being laid off from my job as a government writer, which happened on my youngest daughter's first birthday. It would have been impossible to find another job that allowed the flexibility to work from home, since it was pre-COVID, letting us continue juggling the girls between us—my husband, an afternoon sitter (because hubby worked nights) and me—to accommodate our work schedules. Because we didn't have the girls in daycare, I was left scrambling, trying to figure out how to bring in an income with two diaper-butts running around the house. Against my better judgment, but somehow with a gut feeling that this was the best option, I turned to entrepreneurship.

With my daughters watching, I built my business from freelance writing to book coaching and editing to a full publishing house over the course of several years. When I wanted to give up (because, honestly, this is flipping hard!), I was inspired to show my daughters that you really can have a career you enjoy and also be a mom.

I remember how miserable I was at my corporate job when they were really little and wondering how I could teach them to seek out a career that lights them up without being a hypocrite. Starting my own business was the answer, though it's been a bumpy and chaotic ride!

Seasoned moms know that there is nothing we can't do because we've been doing it for years! (Run a business, run a marathon, raise kids, get a massage, and be an amazing wife? It'll take some juggling, but we will figure it out.) The women in this book want to help inspire business owners who are also mothers to become the powerful leaders they want to be *because* they are mothers.

It's crazy how having children and stepping into the role of motherhood gives us a little edge in our own lives. It's something

Introduction

that maybe we didn't expect, but it's allowed us to be the leaders we were truly meant to be!

The women in this book have beautiful stories about how being in the trenches has allowed them to come out stronger and paved their true divine-given path, leading to their passion work. Going through that, while being a mom, has made them into the people they are today. They have changed and grown, adapted and pivoted to take their businesses where they want them to go. And *because* they are moms, they found their way.

And you can too.

Women business owners who have flourished because they became mothers are finally sharing their stories about—

- How they found balance
- How they allowed themselves grace
- How they pushed through their challenges
- What others can learn from their truths

And most of all, how their growing families inspired them through all of this!

Sharing a personal story can be challenging when you're trying to do it on your own, so we have joined forces to create a beautiful synergy that led to a powerful compilation of stories with a shared purpose: uplifting others and giving them hope.

We hope that you gain so much from this book, created through the power of moms coming together for a purpose. Through the stories we share here, we hope you see that we get your challenges, but we are also shining a light on the other side, on the best parts of being a mom and business owner at the same time. For those moms out there struggling, we hope this light is a positive glow that you keep an eye on through the darkest of times!

As mothers, we can do anything we put our minds to! And we want to positively impact the next generation. Enjoy these stories of triumph over our challenges!

Foreword

Marta Sauret Greca

On my heart, I have always had the tug to share the truth via entrepreneurship that we can have it all and do it all, and at the same time, choose when to be all in and when to pause and rest and give ourselves space. This is how motherhood and entrepreneurship can both unfold alongside each other, lifting each other up. My mission is to debunk the myth that once we become mothers, our life is over, and we are to put ourselves on the back burner as we live our lives in servitude to others. Instead, I like to encourage moms to take care of themselves, ask for help, and instead, understand that at the root of their families' success lies their own health and happiness. That instead of us being the one person who pours ourselves empty for everyone and sacrifices our own goals and dreams for the joy of others, we can serve our families *and* businesses as a benevolent leader who asks others for help and allows others to serve *us*. That with every baby, we can actually grow into more success and an even better running business, and that with each step of business growth, there's increased opportunity to be even more present for ourselves and truly live our best lives.

That is what this book is about. When Cori approached me, it was easy to land on this theme.

However, I had a totally different story I was going to share when, as we neared deadlines for the first draft, and I had my schedule and timeline and goals perfectly planned out, our seventh baby, a boy, was born a month early! I knew I had to share our family's story around it; I felt compelled. It was a perfect example of the theme in this book—that an unforeseen perceived derailment can actually lead us to our destined path.

Powerful Synergy

At times it feels silly to share a story that pales in comparison to those who have been through it "way worse." But I hope my own anecdote and those of others in this book inspire you to share your own stories and encourage you to know that your own experiences and your feelings pertaining to them are more than valid.

I am so grateful for the inspiring women entrepreneurs who stepped forward to collaborate on this project and share their own stories. Each chapter is as incredible as the woman sharing it. I know you'll enjoy each and every one.

Maverick Moments

Marta Sauret Greca

"You're not supposed to be here."

"I know. It's just ... I'm just honestly about to have a nervous breakdown between trying to be with my baby and being where I'm supposed to be, and it's all a lot."

I couldn't see who was talking, but the scenario felt very familiar to me as I overheard this conversation. I could only assume it was a fellow neonatal intensive care unit (NICU) mom wanting to see her baby and a medical professional talking to her, encouraging her to go back to her room, while reminding her she needs to take care of herself, too. Doing so would be best for her and her family.

I had just snuck into one of the overnight-sleeper-rooms for NICU parents before check-in time so I could use one of the private bathrooms rather than waiting, once again, in line with a nearly bursting bladder—or worse—trying *not* to overly listen-in and allow this mom the privacy she was probably seeking, while she was hiding out in a private bathroom.

I'd already had my own breakdown as a mom who'd just delivered her premature baby via an unexpected, emergency C-section and having my own baby in the NICU days after I'd been discharged from the hospital. I could relate to the voice of the woman being coaxed back into the area where she was "supposed to be."

It's a common scenario for moms as they await the release of their brand new babies into their arms: this battle between being "where you're supposed to be" which is either in your own hospital room healing, hooked up to some monitors, or quite frankly any other possible scenario among the hospital's 90 different families being cared for in the NICU and being with your baby.

It's also common to feel conflicted by the feelings that you have as you're being wheeled around, hopped up on pain killers, being congratulated for a new birth that almost feels like part of a loss.

It was just a week prior that I was 36 weeks pregnant, thinking I was working ahead in my business at my dining room table—about to hit record for a new Instagram reel for a brand—when all of a sudden, a pain shot throughout my entire lower back and into my pelvis, sending chills down my thighs and glutes and into my arms, leaving me with only the ability to scream through the pain.

"Call 911!" I yelled through the brief moment I could muster up some words between the screams.

But after an ambulance ride to the nearest hospital, the pain had subsided, and the contractions that came thereafter subsided as well. With no other labor signs and since baby's heartbeat seemed to be good, they sent me back home.

It wasn't until over 48 hours later that the contractions came back with a vengeance—every five minutes with no reprieve in between—so we went to the hospital again. While we all assumed this was another case of false labor, treated with a few hours of monitoring the contractions again, it was revealed that my baby's heartbeat was dropping with each one. And after a final excessive drop, medical professionals rushed in, filling every corner of the room, checking what felt like every possible connection and crevice in a moment's time.

"He's not OK. We have to get him out now," said one of the doctors that I'd just met for the very first time.

"OK," is all I could say in response.

"I'm glad you agree," she answered, slightly surprised.

"Well, it doesn't sound like we have much of a choice," I said with an ironic chuckle.

Later, my husband teased me about my one-word, matter-of-fact response, "Ok," to which I joked back, "What should I have said? 'No, thank you! We were planning on a home birth, actually.'"

And with that, we were rushed toward the operating room (OR), as I let the knot in my throat turn into the tears I had been holding back. I listened to the medical team debate which form of anesthesia we actually had time for.

Within minutes, I was in the OR, curtains up to shield the surgery, numbed from the waist down, and cut open.

And within seconds after that, one of the medical professionals yelled, "Abruption! Abruption!"

This yelling signaled what my midwife had already suspected days earlier, that the mind-numbing pain I experienced was a placental detachment, leading to internal bleeding-out for me, and meaning that my baby boy was no longer receiving any blood supply or nutrition needed for him to remain alive inside the womb.

"Time of birth: 6:26 a.m.!"

And still ... no baby's cry.

No familiar feeling of someone immediately placing the baby on my chest or in my arms like I'd gotten to experience with our previous six babies' births.

Just silence, leaving my husband and me to look at each other in shock, wondering if our baby was even alive.

Is he OK? I kept wondering, trying to express the words with my mouth.

Minutes later, a doctor walked over to let us know he was stable, and that they'd let us see him soon.

He was wheeled past me head, and I was able to see my tiny boy through an open Plexiglas bassinet. They went by so quickly, just long enough to say *hello*, and then he was whisked off again to the NICU to get him further help breathing.

They transferred my husband and me into a completely separate recovery room.

Powerful Synergy

I texted my family and friends.

"Maverick was born at 6:26 a.m. via emergency C-section. He is now stable in NICU—prayers welcome."

The congratulatory messages poured in.

But it didn't feel like a congratulatory moment. My husband and I just sat in silence next to each other, until they came in to let us know we could see him.

My eyes widened, as I choked up through my words, "Me, too?"

"Yep! You can see him too! We'll get you into a wheelchair to visit him before we transfer you into your room for the next few days."

I wish I could tell you who said what and when. But in this scenario, I felt like there were new faces, specialists, and news coming at us in what felt like dozens per minute.

When they brought us to him, he was in a clear Plexiglas incubator, hooked up to breathing tubes coming out of his little nose, and a thin red string of feeding tubes into his little mouth. On his tiny feet, there were IVs hooked up to easily transmit medicine and fluids, as needed.

We put our hands through the designated hand slots on each side of the incubator, my husband standing opposite of me, and we each took one of his hands into ours on our respective sides.

This was one of the few times I'd ever seen my husband cry.

At the moment, I couldn't understand why he was crying. I was just so happy my baby was alive, and that I was getting to see him and touch him for the first time.

But my own breakdown came days later, when at the last minute of thinking we could take him home, they notified us that his blood work didn't come back as favorably as hoped, which meant that he'd be staying at the NICU indefinitely, even though I'd been discharged to go home.

I found myself feeling like Tom Hanks in the movie *The Terminal*—stuck in a large, expansive commercial facility, doing what I could to find food and keep up with my ravishing appetite around the cafeteria's and cafe's odd hours. I did everything I could to pump and breastfeed 24/7, which was one of the very few things I *could* do for my baby boy.

In these times, I became one of the mommy zombies—wisps of hair falling out of loose buns, loose clothes to ensure they don't press on all the sensitive bits left from our birth stories—a shift in mindset came to the rescue, reminding me to focus on the good, to stay in gratitude, and look for the helpers. I needed it when every day felt like it could be the day my baby comes home with me, and then turned out to not be that day at all.

I sat, literally, almost 24/7, tethered by monitor adhesives attached to my baby's chest, leading to a screen of lines and beeps that monitored his oxygen and heartbeat. I was unable—and at moments, unwilling—to stray more than a few feet from my baby's various sleeping cots. (They changed according to his medical needs that day.)

Even though we were some of the lucky ones—my husband and I both being business owners, we already had business models that allowed us to be with our kids most days—I still broke down when they told us we needed to stay at the NICU. We divided and conquered which meant I could be at the NICU all day, every day while my husband stayed home with our other six kids and tried to work with them in tow.

That breakdown was the moment that I decided to truly focus on the good: the good that we were there for just a few days because Maverick's prognosis was much milder than other babies. He spent every other day under blue lights to lower his bilirubin levels and heated incubators to regulate his consistently dropping temperature. Continued blood work monitored his hemoglobin and reticulocyte levels, and his liver functions progressed positively each day.

Right next to him, daily, I overheard the doctors as they did their rounds. They would say things like, *This is (so and so). This baby has been here for 49 days.* Or *This is so and so. This is baby's 60th day in the NICU.* These were babies that day in and day out needed to remain in their bassinets or incubators, only leaving them every three hours to be held and fed and changed, or in more severe cases, not even having such privileges. They slept soundly except for the moments when they were cared for, letting out little cries as they were poked and prodded, followed by routine bottle feedings by the nurses assigned to them for that 12-hour stretch.

I prayed for those babies and their families and felt guilty for being grateful that Maverick had been allowed off his feeding and breathing tubes and IVs within just a day or so of being in the NICU, and I'd been allowed to hold him and nurse him pretty much on demand not long after. I'd had the privilege to stay at the hospital 24/7 and hadn't exited the campus since the moment we walked in the night before he was born.

I decided to focus on these exact bits of gratefulness that lifted me from the desperation: the pining to be home in my bed with my new baby and the rest of the kids by my side, and turning that desperation into accepting this as the current reality. Shifting my focus allowed me to witness all the good in the unknown.

I focused on being grateful for the angels on earth we call NICU nurses, who not only juggle dozens and dozens and dozens (and beyond) of miniature babies but also manage the just as numerous waves of emotions coming from the NICU parents on a daily basis.

The same shifts in mindset that have served me in the decade-plus long journey riding the rollercoaster of entrepreneurship as a mom, were the same ones getting me through the rollercoaster of this experience.

When highlight moments unexpectedly turn into unfavorable outcomes, or when projections don't quite pan out as hoped, or when, instead of living in the present moment, we let our minds wander into what could be in the future, in these moments the shifts in mindset are EVERYTHING to keep an entrepreneur going. They literally save our lives.

And vice versa—as I sat and had hours to think in the NICU, I noticed how the rollercoaster of motherhood and the ability that child-bearing women who are CEOs of their own brands have to weather the storms for their babies, allow us to hold our heads high and our shoulders strong for our clients and business.

In this scenario, I was beyond grateful for all of the hypnotherapy, Rapid Transformation Therapy (RTT), meditating, mindset coaching, divine readings, and, you name it, that I'd devoured over the past half-decade to move from surviving into thriving in entrepreneurship and that these were the very same things getting me through these difficult moments with my family.

Instead of fixating on *being stuck at the NICU*, I framed it as being grateful for having the freedom and support to be here so I could hold my baby as much as possible.

Instead of focusing on being surrounded by medical staff 24/7 and viewing it as an intrusion of privacy from what would otherwise be an intimate home birth and endless cuddles in my own home, I thanked God for the round-the-clock care that doubled as support with changing diapers and feeding my baby when I was lucky enough to get a private sleeper room down the hall and to go get some rest.

Instead of having an uncontrollable desire to only be in my own bedroom with my kids, I sent texts to my friends when I won the proverbial lottery of private sleeper rooms that came equipped with its own full bath and even windows! (With the NICU's capacity of 90 babies, they only have the ability to host four sets of parents in their sleeper rooms per night.)

Instead of wishing I was home being cooked for by my husband with his awesome skills, I was so very grateful for the three-course, nine dollar trays the service staff delivered right to the NICU lobby, or the godsend called Christopher's Kitchen—a room stocked with food for families at the hospital supporting their little ones, allowing us to stay nearby or feed ourselves in the middle of the night.

Instead of chastising myself for not having anything at all to dress my unexpected early arrival in, I was grateful for the basket of adorable preemie clothes available for moms just like me.

Instead of having guilt about not being able to do what I'd normally do as Mom for our six older kids if I were home, I focused on how grateful I was for their resilience in rising to the occasion of autonomy. I was amused to hear that even though for Mom, it was like pulling teeth most mornings to get them out of the house on time, they were able to individually get themselves ready and off to school on their own, and in the cases of the older children, help with dinner or homework or laundry or anything else their dad needed help with.

And when I would have given anything for clean clothes after a three-day stretch of having run out of them, and my husband being unable to bring me any (he was already juggling his business and six kids at home, which was a good hour away from the hospital, depending on the time of the day), I cherished the jovial conversations I had with the information desk clerk named Malcom. Malcom walked the entire hospital with me until we'd found the single article of clothing the shopper on my phone app actually found me from a nearby store. Malcom even offered to bring clothes from his own home if my family couldn't bring me any the next day. And told me his own story of overnight stays at another children's hospital with his own son.

I was so grateful for understanding clients and colleagues as my administrative team reached out to cancel and reschedule everything, push back deadlines, and rework timelines and goals. I was grateful for sticking to my standards and boundaries toward those who weren't as understanding.

I was grateful for the skills I'd learned through entrepreneurial leadership to speak up and tell those around me how I was really feeling and what was really needed in moments when one would otherwise smile and say, "I'm OK" or "that's OK" when OK is far from what's being experienced.

Thankful doesn't begin to describe my feelings toward the friends and family who brought me sushi, my favorite lattes, clothes for the baby, and diapers to last us months and months. (We received a literal mountain of diapers from my local mom group that brought me to tears in the most awesome way).

Every day I thanked God for the team members who were totally taking over for me with communication, delegation, and project completion in my business, even going above and beyond managing schedules and to do lists and issuing reminders to help me function during this hectic time.

It truly is a beautiful marriage between motherhood and entrepreneurship, one complimenting the other. There is a myth making its way around the world that if you want to be present for one, the other needs sacrificed.

But that really isn't the case.

Because of motherhood, entrepreneurship can become that much more successful. Our kids and their needs fuel us to keep going, and at the same time, our kids are our biggest *whys* for having strong boundaries against over-giving or overextending in times when we need to pause and rest.

Conversely, entrepreneurship allows us the freedom to be there for our kids when we want to be and the inspiration to be all-in when our business lights us the "F" up.

And both experiences allow us to become clearer regarding our missions, our passions, and our messaging toward what we truly want to communicate and contribute to the world with our gifts.

An emergency C-section was not on my radar after six birth stories that had gone almost completely well. But having been on the ever-winding entrepreneurial road and learning to seek the support and healing necessary to keep moving forward, and pausing and resting to weather the storms, was truly lifesaving during such an ordeal. And conversely, going through this experience allowed me to keep my family at the forefront and stay focused on my vision for my business, while understanding that everything happens in its own time, as it should.

It allowed me to experience more deeply the truth behind fully consented care and the importance of braiding holistic health with traditional medical care to treat the whole human and their family. I always say, *God didn't give me the freedom to heal people, but He sure as heck gave me the gift to help the healers market themselves, so we can continue to share the truth about true beauty and wellness.*

A few days after my son's birth, being that he wasn't due for another four weeks, I was meant to take one last test for my professional expansion and growth-path toward getting a license to sell retirement products such as Roth IRAs and 529 plans, adding to my existing licensure for selling life insurance. Because of what I'd learned in my years as an entrepreneur, I didn't worry about missing it and just contacted my team for support on canceling the exam and reopening my testing dates. Going through this experience, once again, strengthened my passion for supporting families, their financial wellbeing, and freedom through disposable income and entrepreneurship. My role as a financial representative and insurance representative will allow me to build a team to help others be entrepreneurs, serving the world as well.

Throughout it all, no matter what I do professionally, at the core will always be the subliminal message of family. Every life is such a miracle, and we have the power as women to build a career that allows us to be as present as we want to be with the miracles we bring into the world. Every moment in entrepreneurship is an opportunity to put family at the forefront, allowing it to propel your success forward and vice versa. They go hand in hand. One does not hinder the other, and both unpredictable journeys will certainly teach you lessons that will bring a wealth of wisdom.

And when it feels like parenthood might necessitate a reprieve from full-on focus in your business, trust in God that, no matter what, you are provided for, and God's divine economy is everlasting. His bounty is overflowing for you exactly how you need it, no matter the scenario our human lives may be presented with.

Maverick was discharged after just nine days in the NICU, once his temperature self-regulated, his bilirubin levels seemed manageable, and his liver seemed to be functioning properly. He has been growing steadily from his five pounds, ten ounces birthweight and required minimal regular follow-up and routine blood work. Otherwise, he has experienced great health.

To this day I am still meeting so many parents with wondrous NICU stories. Parents who were there for months with their babies, born way earlier and smaller than mine, sharing their triumphs of now adult individuals living their best lives, which I am so happy to hear.

Maverick's name was chosen before his journey ever unfolded itself before us, and I'm not surprised that it fits so perfectly as another nudge from what I like to think is God's sense of humor for us sometimes. And Maverick, like his six siblings, has been yet another beautiful reminder that God is truly in charge and that, through hardships, important lessons are learned and the most amazing opportunities to fully surrender into the present moment flourish.

And of course, just like every other one of our children, Maverick, along with his six brothers and sisters, continues to inspire more divine guidance for our businesses. Our kids are a constant encouragement for which paths to take.

About Marta

Marta Sauret Greca is the CEO of MEDIA - The Creative Agency, a marketing agency that helps holistic wellness and beauty experts.

Marta has been named "Woman Business Leader of the Year" by the Pittsburgh North Regional Chamber of Commerce. Her book, *The Minimalist Method: The Emerging Entrepreneur's Guide to Peace and Prosperity*, is a number one bestseller. She has been featured in national media outlets like KDKA, WPXI, *The Today Show* blog, and *Inspiring Lives Magazine*.

As someone who emigrated from Italy at nine years old, Marta has citizenship in Italy, France, and the United States. She takes pride in having created a business that provides projects for many creatives in the United States, as an immigrant.

Her favorite thing to do in the entire world is to travel with her family and have fun outdoors, most importantly with her seven kids, her Aussiedoodle M, their chickens, and all the wildlife on their beautiful sprawling lakeside property in Pennsylvania.

She is always game to be a contributing expert on upcoming shows internationally or a speaker at your upcoming event.

Connect with Marta

You can follow along with more of Maverick's and his brothers' and sisters' lives and Marta's professional news through Marta's Instagram @martasauretgreca.

Hustling for Survival

Tanya Bashor

When I first arrived in America, I was a young woman in love and brimming with hopes and dreams. The vast Atlantic Ocean separated me from my family and friends and the familiar comforts of my home in England. As they say, hindsight is 20/20, and, looking back on it all now (through a trauma-informed lens), I realize I wasn't running toward someone, I was actually running away from my trauma.

After my first divorce at age 22, and another traumatic breakup after a two-year relationship with the man I thought I would spend the rest of my life with, I came to the United States to work as a nanny. I cared for the children of a defenseman for the Pittsburgh Penguins hockey team. I felt compelled to leave my small town as everyone knew all the sordid details of my divorce. I told myself I needed a fresh start, but I was actually dissociated and numbing the pain by running away to America.

My intention was to work in the United States for one year and then return to England once all the drama had blown over. But I met Mr. Wonderful and relocated here permanently for *love*. In the beginning, when we were both partying hard, it was all fun and games: plenty of love, laughter, and good times. Looking back now, I realize that I was codependent, and he had narcissistic tendencies. Codependents love to give until it hurts, and narcissistic people take until it hurts. It was a perfect match ... until it wasn't! After a couple of years, we decided to have a child, and things changed. I grew up and became a responsible adult, but my spouse continued to drink. I was in that toxic marriage for 22 long years. Our relationship was a tumultuous roller coaster with bouts of emotional turmoil and fear, and my body was in a relentless struggle of fight, flight, freeze. I left him

Powerful Synergy

four times, each departure a desperate attempt for a better life. Amidst the pain and chaos, my two children were my beacons of hope—the reason I got up each morning to face the day. They deserved a stable, nurturing environment, and I was determined to provide that, no matter the cost or how long it took.

In those early years, my life was exhausting. Not only was I fighting nonstop with my husband—who did very little to help with the daily care of our child—I had to drop my son off at a family daycare before work, drive an hour into the city, work eight hours, and then drive an hour back home, picking him up from daycare on my way back from work (even though my husband finished work two hours before me!). In the evenings, I would sometimes need to swing by the grocery store, then cook dinner, squeeze in some housework, bathe my son, put him to bed, and get up and do the same thing again the next day. On the weekends, I cleaned the house, grocery shopped, paid the bills, and did the laundry. I did that for over two years, and I was physically, emotionally, and mentally exhausted.

Eventually, it took its toll, and I gave up a well-paid corporate job to stay home and raise my son. I cashed in my 401(k) so we didn't have a car payment, and we lived on one salary for a while. The traditional nine-to-five job was not an option for me, especially after I had my daughter, as it wouldn't allow me the flexibility to be there for both of my children when they needed me most. Instead, I turned to entrepreneurship. I desperately needed to make my own money so I could figure out a way to leave my toxic marriage.

I was a self-employed nanny for many years when my children were very young as it allowed me to take them to work. I could care for them and my charges (the children I cared for) while being paid. I also tried my hand at various direct sales ventures—each one teaching me invaluable lessons about running a business, sales and marketing, resilience, and the importance of never giving up. For three years, I worked seasonally, selling Christmas tchotchkes and decorations. I scheduled parties in the evening (back in the day when house parties were popular) and left for them once my husband got home from work. I'd load up my car on the weekends with battery-operated singing Santa toys and other such novelties and present my wares for groups of women. I was always the upbeat saleswoman, brimming with festive cheer, using it as a mask to hide the pain of my miserable marriage. While it didn't make me rich, it did put gifts under our tree. The smiles on my children's faces on Christmas morning made every late night worth it.

Next, I ventured into the world of loose tea. I loved the idea of bringing a bit of my English heritage to my new community. I sold the finest teas and accessories, but this business didn't take off as I had hoped. As with many direct-sales positions, I bought more than I sold. Tea wasn't as popular back then as it is nowadays. It did, however, stir up a dream of one day owning my own tearoom, and I spent hours scouring thrift stores searching for bone china teacups and teapots and three-tiered trays. I baked a mean scone and dreamed of someday hosting bridal showers and mother-daughter teas in an old house with a large wooden porch somewhere in the suburbs. This dream helped distract me from my toxic marriage. Over the years, I collected a dozen large bins full of everything I would need to open a tearoom—from golden teaspoons to cake plates—and I moved those containers with me every time I left my husband! Even though the shopping was a trauma response at the time (I'm aware of that now), I'm still not ready to give up fully on this dream.

I then moved on to a craft business, channeling my creativity into making handmade wreaths and flower arrangements, pouring my heart into every piece. The crafting community was welcoming and supportive, but financial stability still seemed out of reach.

Once my children were older, I went back into the workforce and quickly got promoted through the ranks in banking. I finally had a stable income and with it came the opportunity to leave my husband and support myself and my kids.

I also flipped furniture before the days of TikTok! While working at the bank I worked odd jobs for cash and did whatever I needed to do to scrape together enough money for a security deposit on an apartment so that I could leave my marriage. Eventually, after leaving for the fourth time, I did indeed leave for good and file for divorce.

In 2018, I entered and won a business pitch competition, and Gypsy Artistry was born. It was a successful pop-up crafting business where women could meet at wine bars and restaurants and create a craft while chatting away with one another. The pandemic hit, and I closed the business. But, through that venture, one thing became abundantly clear—I had a knack for connecting with people, especially women who were going through hardships similar to mine. They saw in me a kindred spirit, someone who had faced the fire and come out stronger. During one of these heart-to-heart conversations with a friend who was a high-performance coach (while the COVID-19 pandemic was in full swing), the idea for my trauma-informed coaching business, Impart Clarity LLC, was born.

The journey to start Impart Clarity was not without its challenges. I had no formal training in coaching, and I was plagued by self-doubt and fears. Who was I to offer advice to others when my own life had been so messy and chaotic? But then I realized that my life experiences were indeed all the credentials I needed. I had lived through the very situations I wanted to help other women overcome. My empathy and understanding came from a place of genuine connection and shared pain. I could connect and empathize authentically. That was a great start, but I knew I needed to get an actual certification as a trauma-informed coach.

I began to educate myself on domestic abuse, financial abuse, trauma, healing, and resilience. I completed a 12-month certification and became a Certified Narcissistic Trauma

Informed Coach™. I read many books on cognitive behavioral therapy (CBT), complex PTSD, polyvagal theory (highlighting the role of the vagus nerve in regulating stress), as well as numerous books on the impact of trauma caused by narcissistic abuse. I attended workshops and online trainings and gradually built the knowledge base I needed to support my clients effectively. I decided that my coaching practice would primarily focus on helping women recover from the effects of toxic relationships and financial abuse, guiding them toward a life of empowerment, fulfillment, and financial security.

One of the most rewarding aspects of my work has been seeing the transformation in the women I coach. They come to me broken, their self-esteem shattered by years of emotional abuse and manipulation. Together, we work through their pain, uncovering the strength they didn't know they had. My role is not to give them the answers but to help them find their own paths to healing and happiness. I wish I'd had someone like that myself when I was going through the same thing.

I often share my story with them, not for sympathy, but to show them that recovery and success are possible. I tell them about the dark days when I too felt like giving up and the small victories that kept me going. I remind them that a failed marriage or relationship is not the end but is often a path to something greater.

As my children grew older and more independent, I poured more of my energy into Impart Clarity. I began hosting workshops and retreats, creating safe spaces where women could come together, share their stories, and support each other. These retreats have been transformative, not just for the participants, but for me as well. Seeing these women blossom into confident, empowered individuals has been the most fulfilling part of my journey as an entrepreneur.

Looking back, I can honestly say that I am grateful for every challenge and setback. Every unsuccessful business venture taught me something new and brought me closer to my true

Powerful Synergy

calling. Those experiences, and hustling for survival, shaped me into the woman I am today and gave me the tools to help others. My story is not just about survival, but about thriving in the face of adversity. It is a testament to the power of resilience and the importance of following your dreams, no matter how impossible they may seem.

In fact, just ask my kids—they are living proof. My son, now a successful lawyer, often reminds me that my perseverance and unwavering love set the foundation for his achievements. My daughter's adventures in Spain, teaching English and exploring new cultures, fill me with pride. They are both evidence that breaking free from a toxic environment can open doors to a brighter future.

Until recently, I was still working a full-time corporate job and running my coaching business on the side—as more of a hobby, truth be told. I struggled with trusting myself enough to make a living out of my business. But one day, after listening to too many employee complaints and realizing what a toxic workplace I was in, I did something very uncharacteristic: I voted for myself. I sent my boss an email to let her know that I quit, and I walked out, leaving a high-paying career behind. I am now going all-in on myself and my business as a full-time trauma recovery coach. I plan to host large-scale retreats, as just one way to reach more women. My entrepreneurial story is still being written, and I am absolutely positive that the best chapters are yet to come.

To the young mothers who feel trapped in their circumstances, I say this: *Never give up on your dreams.* The road may be long and full of all kinds of obstacles, but every step you take brings you closer to your goal. If one thing doesn't work, don't be afraid to try something else. Your resilience is—without question—your greatest asset. And with it, you can achieve anything you set your mind to. The path to entrepreneurship is never a straight one. There are many bends in the road, and you may pivot a few times before landing on what resonates with you and what can be a successful business. And that is perfectly OK! The keys are to never take your eyes off the goal of entrepreneurship and never give up!

About Tanya

Tanya Bashor is the founder and CEO of Impart Clarity LLC, where she specializes in providing education and coaching to those affected by trauma from narcissistic abuse. Through her free Facebook community, educational blog, diverse coaching programs, and immersive retreats, Tanya offers a comprehensive support system to help people heal and thrive. Having personally overcome narcissistic trauma, she ensures that her clients feel genuinely heard and understood, guiding them to regain their confidence and rediscover their joy. Tanya resides in Pittsburgh with her husband, Fred, and enjoys

Powerful Synergy

kayaking and biking. She has two adult children, and a sweet black lab named Bella.

Connect with Tanya

Learn how Tanya can help you heal after a toxic relationship by visiting https://linktr.ee/ImpartClarity

Wherever You Go

Samantha Bauer

"Have I not commanded you? Be strong and courageous. Do not be afraid; do not be discouraged, for the Lord your God will be with you wherever you go." Joshua 1:9 (NIV)

Why do some women desire to work at building a career and some women desire to be a stay-at-home parent? Why do some women desire both things? And why the *bleepity, bleep, bleep* does society tell us that we have to choose one or the other?

As a God-fearing, career-loving mom, I believe that whatever is in your heart to pursue was put there by the one who created you as well as everything in, on, and around this planet. And it was put there for a reason. God doesn't give us dreams and desires if we weren't meant to pursue them. I believe that God created every human life *on* purpose and *for* a purpose and that not a hair falls out of our heads, but by the will of God.

If your desire is to serve God by serving your family and being a stay-at-home parent, you need to figure out a way to do that. If your desire is to charge forth in a career that you love and where you can shine your light on others outside of your home, you need to figure out a way to do that. And momma, if your desire is to do both, to be a loving and present spouse and mother to your family and to have a career, you need to figure out a way to do that!

Yes! Go get it! But, how?

I so often hear the advice *to follow your dreams, become the person that God created you to be*, but there's no manual on how to actually do these things. You might want to stay home, but maybe you need to make money. You might want to work full time, but your kids are home and they need things like being fed, having diapers changed, being read to, and being loved.

Powerful Synergy

They need a momma who is present for them. So, the answer that most people have come up with over the years is that you have to choose. Do you want to be a mom, or do you want a career? Because you can't have both, sister.

I'm here to tell you that is a bunch of bullpucky!

When I started my business five years ago, I honestly wasn't sure where I was being led, but I was very confident that God was calling me to become a business owner. I had been in a corporate career for 15 years and had been quite successful. I was in a senior leadership position with a large team and all the perks: the corner office, the corporate card, and a very comfortable paycheck every other week. It also came with an abundance of stress, a toxic work environment, lots of time away from my family, and unreasonable expectations.

My kids were five and six years old, and unfortunately, I'd become a very part-time mom and an even more part-time spouse to my husband. Quite honestly, they were all fine. When I was home for those ten waking hours per week, I was able to be as present as possible because my husband was a stay-at-home parent at the time (which he loved and thrived at!) Also, we were comfortable financially.

But one day it dawned on me—I was not happy. I loved my career, but I loved my family more. I realized that ninety percent of my energy and time were going to a career within a large corporation that doesn't even share my values, and I knew I had to make a change. But how? I was the sole provider for my family. I worked for 15 years to get a senior leadership role in my company. Could I really leave it now to start over somewhere else? And what would I do? How will my husband react when I bring up that he might have to leave the role he loves so much and go back to work? Is this what is best for my kids after they've gotten used to the lifestyle this job has provided?

I just couldn't see how I could leave my corporate job.

I started to pray about it. I prayed every day on my way to work for over a year. I cried. I pleaded with God, "Please Lord, I will do whatever work you give me today, and I will work for man as though I am working for you, but please God, open my eyes to what you are calling me to because I just can't believe that this is it."

"Hey God, if you could just show me what you want me to do, I'll do it!"

"Ummm ... God? Me again. Are you there? I'm still here doing this awful job and hating it. Please tell me you have another plan for me?"

This went on and on and on. (When we are waiting for this big sign from God, time. Stands. Still.)

I was so frustrated and couldn't figure out why God hadn't dropped a solution in my lap. One night, I came home in tears, and I finally told my husband what had been going on—how unhappy I was—and just dumped it all on him. He looked at me like he always does and said, "Sam, I'll do whatever I need to do to support your next move. Let's pray about it."

We held hands and prayed together that night, and then, knowing that I had his support, I started to take steps to leave that job. I researched different opportunities. I looked at some new job possibilities, but I also had this desire in my heart to own my own business. So, I explored a bunch of different business options as well.

After a few months, I came to the realization that my career in insurance had afforded me a deep knowledge of how the insurance industry works and how to lead people and high performing teams. I have always possessed the gift of communication, which is what I believe to be the number one requirement for being a good salesperson. Together, my husband and I determined that opening my own insurance agency made the most sense and would also help create an income within three to five years that would put me back to what I was earning in my corporate career. My husband quickly found a job that would cover our expenses until we got our feet on the ground, and I opened my agency in May of 2019.

Powerful Synergy

Now, a few things happen when you start taking action on the desires of your heart in a prayerful way.

First, God starts providing. Turns out all that prayer I had been doing started coming to fruition when I began taking steps in faith that God would provide. Turns out, prayer isn't just *Ask and you shall receive* all the time. Sometimes (I think most of the time), you need to pray *and* take action. Taking the action is like saying, *Hey God, I trust that you heard me, so I'm going to get to work so you can too.* Sometimes God can't provide the answers because you aren't doing anything yet, and His answers won't be helpful until you are actually taking the steps required to begin your journey toward who you want to become.

The second thing that happens is that the devil becomes angry. He does not want us to become the people God created us to be. He doesn't want us to be closer to our families, doesn't want us to be fully present for our kids and spouses. He doesn't want us to have more time to serve our communities or our churches, and he certainly doesn't want us to inspire others to do the same. The devil wants us frustrated and overworked and irritable; he wants us to be so consumed with things of this world that we can easily be manipulated into turning our backs on what is truly important in this life. He will do everything he can to get you to *not* become who God created you to be because that person is a threat to all the things that the devil loves.

Fear, self-doubt, distrust, unbelief—none of these things come from God. And if they do not come from God, they come from his enemy.

I should have been certain that I was doing exactly what God wanted me to do because in that first year of my business, the devil came at me hard.

My daughter became so ill with complicated pneumonia that we spent 14 days over Christmas in Children's Hospital watching her fight for her life through multiple lung surgeries. God saved her, and my business allowed me to be in that hospital room every day and every night and not miss a second with her.

I miscarried a baby a couple of weeks later. It was the hardest thing I've ever experienced. God sat with me, and my business allowed me to work from home while I recovered emotionally and physically from the surgery and continued to work.

COVID hit a month later and my kids came home from school with all the other kids across the nation. God was with us, and my business allowed me to help them go to their online class sessions while I worked with clients over the phone from home.

I decided to home school my kids during first and second grade in my office because I wasn't sure how my daughter would do in a mask all day after her lung surgeries just six months prior. God blessed us immensely during this year, and I got to spend every day teaching and loving my kids while growing my business ninety percent from the prior year.

Yes, the devil attacks those of us who are pursuing God-ordained dreams. We know how this plays out though; we know who wins the war. By keeping God at the center of all of it, the devil just doesn't stand a chance.

Sometime during the pandemic, I had read an article that someone had posted online. It was written by a woman who couldn't figure it all out. She shared in her article that you simply cannot be a mom and have a career during the pandemic. This article infuriated me mostly because it was a lie—here I was doing exactly what she was telling woman they cannot do. You can be a good mom and have a career! I couldn't believe that just because this woman couldn't figure it out that she'd want to tell other women that they couldn't either. It was in that anger that I promised myself I would figure out how to do both and then do everything I can to share with any momma who will listen how they can do it too.

Start the journey. Take the first step. Start researching, start planning, and don't stop praying. It's not going to be easy, but it's *so* worth it when you build a purposeful life that you love. A life with space for the things that are most important to you.

There will be days when you doubt yourself—remember that doubt does not come from God, and if it doesn't come from God, don't entertain it. Hard things will happen, but you can do hard things.

God will put the right people in the right rooms to help you, but you have to show up in those rooms to meet them. Go build the life you have in your heart, pray all the way, and remember that God's plans might not be the same as yours. I can say with confidence that they almost never happen in the timeframe that you want them to happen. God's timing is funny that way, but try not to trust your feelings in those situations, trust in God. I promise you, He will be with you ... *wherever you go.*

About Samantha

Samantha Bauer

Samantha Bauer is the proud owner of the Bauer Agency - Goosehead Insurance, recently celebrating five successful years in business. She is the president of the Gibsonia Chapter of Christian Business Partners through which she is dedicated to fostering community and collaboration among local Christian entrepreneurs. As a proactive mentor and supporter for fellow business owners, Sam was nominated for the prestigious 2023 Woman Leadership Excellence Award by the North Pittsburgh Chamber of Commerce. Additionally, Sam is the host of the Wherever You Go Podcast and a published author, sharing her insights and experiences to inspire others.

Connect with Samantha

https://www.goosehead.com/agents/pa/allison-park/samantha-bauer/
https://www.facebook.com/GooseheadInsuranceSamanthaBauer

Taking Back Your POWER While Balancing Babies and Business

Emma Ferrick

The worst night of my life set in motion a life I am now profoundly thankful for. In an era where social media often portrays people living a flawless life, enjoying streams of passive income and a picture-perfect motherhood, it's crucial to recognize that this is just a façade and doesn't portray the true struggles of many women striving to be at home with their children while gaining control of their finances. Over the past four years, I've been building my service-based business while facing numerous challenges that could have pushed me to quit. The discomfort, the severe lows, the physical and mental pain, and the fear have all shaped my path to where I am today. Despite everything, I'm grateful to still be on this journey.

It could never happen to me.
I had that thought countless times about being subjected to domestic abuse. Most of us don't go through life expecting to suffer from domestic violence. Yet, according to the World Health Organization, one in three women—approximately 736 million—experience physical or sexual violence by an intimate partner or sexual violence from a non-partner in their lifetime.[1]

---

[1] World Health Organization. "Devastatingly pervasive: 1 in 3 women globally experience violence." 9 March 2021. WHO.
https://www.who.int/news/item/09-03-2021-devastatingly-pervasive-1-in-3-women-globally-experience-violence.

Powerful Synergy

Before enduring an abusive relationship myself, I couldn't comprehend how women found themselves in such situations or why they couldn't leave.

At the young age of 22, I became one of those statistics. Admitting it was the hardest part. Domestic violence can happen to anyone. The statistics show it's more common than we think, but we don't have to let those numbers define us.

How could this happen to me? I thought. I had just graduated college a semester early while unexpectedly pregnant, with a good job, and the support of numerous family members and friends. But none of those achievements made me any less of a statistic. All the good in my life couldn't negate the abuse

I'll never forget the moment my brain registered the brutal reality of what had just happened to me as my head began throbbing and warm blood gushed from my nose. I sat there on the closet floor, holding my blood and ignoring the obscenities he blasted at me. My boyfriend had just hit me in the back of the head with a laundry detergent bottle and violently assaulted me while I lay in the fetal position attempting to protect my head. He screamed at me to "clean myself up and go to bed," snatching my phone so I couldn't call for help. I was in shock, but I had to make a quick decision. My precious, eight-month-old baby girl was asleep in the room across the hall. This wasn't the first time the physical abuse had happened, but I was determined to make sure it was the last. I knew I had to leave to find a safe place for both of us. So, I grabbed my sneakers and left the house at 3 a.m., with no clue of what to do next. It was a defining moment, marking the start of many uphill battles and pushing myself through discomfort.

Leaving an abusive relationship is incredibly challenging, due to fears for personal safety, emotional and psychological trauma, financial dependence, social isolation, and legal and custodial challenges. Fear of harm, including physical injury or even the threat of death, keeps many women trapped. Emotional abuse erodes self-esteem and mental health, leading to conditions like depression, anxiety, and post-traumatic stress disorder (PTSD). Financial barriers are significant, as abusers often control the finances, limiting their partner's ability to leave. Social isolation tactics by abusers make it harder to seek help, and navigating the legal system can be daunting and complex.

These obstacles extend beyond the personal realm, profoundly impacting one's professional life. Victims of domestic violence lose a total of eight million days of paid work each year, and between 21–60 percent lose their jobs due to reasons stemming from the abuse, according to the Centers for Disease Control and Prevention.[2] Personally, I missed numerous days of work due to my injuries, being the sole caregiver for my sick child, and attending countless court dates to fight for myself and my daughter. Balancing a corporate nine-to-five job is hard enough as a parent, but being a single parent makes it even more challenging.

I remember one day leaving work to be on time for our custody exchange, only for my daughter to be returned to me over eight hours later because my abuser disregarded the law, despite having visitation rights. This was followed by a trip to our local children's hospital due to false accusations that he made against me of abusing my daughter. I used countless unplanned paid-time-off (PTO) days because of his manipulation tactics. At the time, my job did not offer employees the option to work remotely, making the situation even more difficult.

Despite these obstacles, I found the strength to reclaim my life. It wasn't easy, but I refused to let the statistics define me as

---

[2] Centers for Disease Control and Prevention, National Center for Injury Prevention and Control. *Costs of Intimate Partner Violence Against Women in the United States*. Atlanta, GA: Centers for Disease Control and Prevention; March 2003.

a struggling single mom. I channeled my experiences and pain into something positive by starting my own business. Determined to never be controlled by anyone again, I focused on providing for both of us, leading to the birth of ELF Operations, my virtual assistant business that would eventually transform into an operations and systems consulting firm. I became passionate about integrating systems, software, and my operations expertise into other women's businesses to help them escape burnout.

Starting my own business unexpectedly led to significant personal healing and inspired connections. Healing would be crucial to my success as a mom and business owner and later as a wife. As uncomfortable as it can be to admit something is wrong with us, it feels incredibly rewarding when you start living a life you never thought possible. But to get there, I had to learn to identify my triggers, calm my nervous system, use coping strategies, accept what had happened, and be OK with a little unknown. These lessons in healing were extremely helpful as I grew my business to new heights and had two more babies.

The biggest trauma response I had to face was overcoming my fear of success. Growing a business tied closely to my personal brand required vulnerability, which, as a trauma survivor, is hard to do. The advice was always to put my face out there, tell my story, go live on social media, cold direct message (DM) people, and go on connection calls. Every time I saw success, I self-sabotaged. I realized I was afraid of what my abuser would do to me or my daughter for sharing my truth and moving forward with my life. I was afraid of letting new people in for fear of being hurt again. But I decided that he would no longer dictate my feelings or my life. I took back my power. That's when things started to take off.

This also led me to deepen my relationship with my now husband, Zach, who has been ELF Operations' greatest supporter and investor! Together, we have pursued entrepreneurship, co-own numerous businesses, and have three beautiful girls. Currently, I'm juggling two under two at home with one in school, and we've realized that a good daycare—even for two days a week—can be a game changer as we stabilize our three businesses and pursue flipping another. Many moms hesitate to admit they need help, but asking for support is essential. I've fought this for so long, trying to do it all myself and making messy mistakes along the way. It is OK and even healthy to ask for support. If you are looking for someone to give you permission, here it is.

I started my business to be home more with my babies, but I realized I needed to advocate for my needs as well. Raising a business, I found, was much like raising a baby. Startups need constant attention, just like newborns. As the mother and the owner, you are the life source—you create it and provide everything it needs. As your baby and business grow, they both start to develop more independence and self-sufficiency. My journey of raising both my children and my business taught me valuable lessons in patience, resilience, and adaptability. ELF Operations is currently only four years old, so if you think about your business as a child, I have a six-year-old, a four-year-old, a two-year-old, and a nine-month-old currently in my home. Hence, my business may not look exactly how I wanted it to because I have leaned into different periods of my life as I needed to. Some days are family focused and some days are business focused.

Through my journey, I've connected with other women who have shared my experiences of domestic violence or longed to be more present for their children's lives. The reasons to give up can be overwhelming. As a mom, we feel the weight of so much on our shoulders: bills, meals, emotional well-being, doctor visits, social calendars, family time, self-care, house cleaning, and more. There have been so many nights I've worked after my girls have gone to bed, sometimes until 4 a.m., to finish client work or cried, stressing over how I could handle working full-time while also being a full-time stay-at-home mom.

Powerful Synergy

As moms, we feel the weight of the world on our shoulders too often. Through my background in process improvement, studies in operations management, and diverse work history (both online and in person), I developed our proven S.I.M.P.L.E framework (for more information, visit my website listed at the end of my chapter) and our three core pillars of focus: Strategy, Systems, and Support. This extends into so many aspects of business and life, even as a mom.

If you're wondering how these three pillars can work for you, let me share one of the many success stories my clients have had. Holly runs a floral business but faced challenges managing its operations. She approached ELF Operations, seeking help with automation without knowing exactly what she needed or how to achieve it. She just knew she wanted to focus on her floral creations and stay in her creative zone of genius. Over four months, we collaborated to transform her business, streamlining processes and implementing new systems that allowed her to scale and grow significantly.

We took a comprehensive approach to understand Holly's business operations, goals, and pain points. Our strategy involves implementing key systems we've discovered most clients, regardless of industry, need to thrive and have time freedom. We introduced a lead management system, client management system, marketing system, and team management system. Some tools I suggest for those looking to get started are HoneyBook, ConvertKit, ClickUp, and Zapier. (For more details about these tools, check out ELF Operations' website resources page.)

With the new systems in place, Holly was able to add two new services, ensuring a steady income stream year-round, not just during the wedding season. By streamlining her services, Holly cut down her administration time by five hours per week. The introduction of ConvertKit led to a thriving monthly email newsletter, driving sales and engagement. Holly also developed a digital product, creating a new passive revenue stream. The combined use of HoneyBook and ClickUp allowed Holly to manage her operations with just an assistant and a social media manager, avoiding the need for additional hires. Despite this lean team, her business grew to over six figures. With the optimized processes, Holly now has more time for personal pursuits, such as planning her upcoming wedding without compromising her business growth.

Holly's transformation is just one example of how strategic systems and support can turn things around. My passion is to help women who feel stuck and in survival mode. Many feel like they don't have control, feel hopeless, and think they can't get out of their situation or that they don't deserve to be happy. I want to inspire these women to take messy action, let go of societal expectations, love themselves, and trust themselves. My goal is to ensure that my three girls—and women everywhere—are not defined by a statistic.

None of this would have been possible if I hadn't found the courage to leave that night after being stuck on the ground. I could have been part of an entirely different statistic, one where reshaping my life would not be possible. I wouldn't have been impacted by these amazing women if I hadn't pushed myself out of survival mode. I also wouldn't have been able to impact so many other women's lives through my work.

The power is within you to take back your personal power. You are worthy of love and a better life. If you're looking for support, please reach out to me. My inbox is always a safe place! You deserve the life of your dreams.

About Emma

Meet Emma Ferrick, the visionary force behind ELF Operations. As an operations and systems strategist, Emma partners with ambitious service providers to implement her S.I.M.P.L.E Ops Framework, the ultimate solution to empower women to break free from survival mode and achieve extraordinary success.

Emma's journey began as a single mother overcoming the challenges of domestic abuse. Determined to build a better life, she founded her business with a focus on automation and efficiency from day one. Today, she inspires and assists women to thrive by implementing effective strategies, systems, and support to achieve their goals and live a life they truly love while also being a mom to three beautiful girls and supporting her husband in his entrepreneurial journey.

Emma's expertise in project scheduling for multi-million-dollar projects and managing online remote teams, combined with her certifications as a verified ClickUp consultant, Lean Six Sigma, and operations management, equips her with unparalleled skills in working with businesses of all sizes. Her mission is to help women gain control over their business and life, enabling them to enjoy the freedom and flexibility they deserve. Join Emma and her Thrive over Survive Mission today!

Connect with Emma

www.elfoperations.com
www.instagram.com/elf_operations
www.linkedin.com/in/emmaferrick

Embracing What You Never Saw Coming

Ashley Fina

I thought those two pink lines would be the biggest surprise of my life, but I had no clue what was coming ...

After many, many thousands of dollars and two rounds of *in vitro* fertilization (IVF), my doctor finally said the words, "It is very unlikely that you will have a biological child. If you'd like to grow your family, you'll have to find another way."

In that moment, I was devastated. But not hopeless.

It was May of 2020, and I was six years into trying.

One of the gifts my years with infertility gave me was a spiritual quest that's still unfolding today. During a meditation, despite all scientific probability telling me otherwise, I got the clearest outline of a little girl. She had blonde curls and blue eyes.

And I knew she was my daughter.

So, I wrote it down and dated the journal August 10, 2020: "I will give birth to a healthy baby girl. She will have blonde curls and blue eyes. She will be full of laughter and joy. And we will learn together about life and meaning. So, it is ..."

Winter came and went, and I held strong to the vision. I stayed in the emotion of seeing this sweet girl, and I let go of the *how*.

I stopped tracking cycles like a maniac and allowed myself to let go of the stranglehold of my dream. I felt more like myself than I had in years. It felt good to be enjoying life, fully present, and doing things I love—*trying to live*, instead of *living to try*.

And one Wednesday morning in March, I took a pregnancy test to get it out of the way. I wondered if I was possibly late. (Remember, I stopped maniacally tracking everything.) I figured I'd rip the Band-Aid off with a big fat negative so I could move on with my day.

Until ... it wasn't negative at all. Those two lines showed up in a hurry.

My heart stopped in disbelief. After six years of nothing but big fat negatives, I had stopped testing until this point. I hated pregnancy tests and the devastation they caused. But this moment was totally different. I squinted. I covered my eyes. I looked again. I thought there must be some sort of mistake. A faulty test messing with me.

After taking a few breaths and pacing around the bathroom, I looked again. Still there. Still positive. This was *really* happening. The best way I can describe what happened inside of me at that moment was confused-icited, nerv-icited, disbelief-icited, and just plain excited!

I never saw this coming.

I walked out of my bathroom to my unexpecting husband minding his own business. I showed him the test, and we laughed. That nervous type of *WTF is happening; life is crazy* laughter that permeated our bedroom until it softened into happy tears and hugs.

My pregnancy carried on in the simplest, most uneventful kind of way. We attended all prenatal appointments, got to see her for the first time at 20 weeks, built her a starry sky nursery, and geeked out over every kick and punch in my belly (and she kicked and punched *a lot*).

I thanked God for this miracle of pregnancy daily. Meanwhile, I leaned into my work as a licensed therapist turned online coach. I built systems to keep my business momentum strong while I was on maternity leave. I had it all figured out: take 12 weeks off, continue to sell my course, come back, and open up slots for one-on-one clients.

Boom! Easy. Simple. Predictable.

But remember when I said that I *thought* those two pink lines would be the biggest surprise of my life? Well, they weren't. That happened on the day I gave birth to my daughter.

She was brand spanking new, and I was desperate to hold and nurse my daughter. To breathe in her features, her smells, her grunts, and her wiggles.

As I begged to hold her immediately after delivery, my pleas were met with silence. Confused about why no one would acknowledge me, minutes felt like hours until a specialist walked in the room.

Finally, I thought! A reasonable person who will give me my baby. But the specialist, too, did not hand her to me. Instead, she told us that this little newborn had all the markers for Down syndrome. Despite all my prenatal testing, no doctor ever brought up concern over her low-bridged nose. They couldn't see her almond shaped eyes or simian crease in the palms of her hands. No one told us about the sandal gap in her toes or the hole in her heart.

I asked the specialist, "How certain are you?"

She answered, "We won't know until the genetic tests come back, but ninety percent."

That moment stood still in time; it just didn't make sense. I was brand new to being a mom and being a mom to a kid with a disability felt like too much for my hormonal heart to hold or my mind to comprehend.

How could my husband and I care for a child with special needs? We didn't know a thing about Down syndrome. We weren't prepared. We weren't equipped. We weren't cut out for it.

All questions lead to the same internal protest: *No! This can't be true. It just can't.*

When I finally got to hold my daughter, I took in her features. She was overwhelmingly beautiful, and I was overwhelmingly scared. All I could think about was how I never saw this coming.

My maternity leave—the one that was supposed to be full of snuggles—was instead full of hospital rooms, surgery, home oxygen tanks, and stress. Not only was she diagnosed with Down syndrome, but she also had significant heart concerns that required immediate attention.

I was madly in love with this child and deeply sad for what she had to endure at the start of her life.

Eventually, her heart got stronger, and the oxygen tank left our home. The stress turned to cuddles and we settled into life with our beautiful girl. Faster than I could comprehend, my maternity leave was over.

I decided to throw myself back into my work, thinking this well-oiled machine would be one thing that would stay predictable. But something felt off. I wasn't the person I was before my daughter was born; yet I wanted to come back to work as if nothing had changed. My *pick up where I left off* plan felt like slogging through quickly drying concrete. I just couldn't do it.

So, I had to get real with myself and do the inner work to truly hear where I was being called next. To build a business that supports my life and not the other way around. To prioritize my values, talents, and freedom above *business as usual*. To be fully present for this new parenting journey and give my young daughter all the support she needs to thrive.

I knew I had to make some changes—big pivots—and it was terrifying. That meant letting go of what I'd worked so hard to build, what I became known for.

But you know the craziest part? This brave decision to pivot ushered me into a new level of business that I would never have predicted. Today, I get to use my love for words and language to help my clients grow their businesses. I get to fully lean into my gifts of writing and communication, along with my psychology background, so business owners can create lifetime customers through their Soul Message. My work is soulful, fulfilling, impactful, and *fun*.

I help business owners bring the right clients into their online world through messaging and copywriting. I never saw that coming. But it makes complete sense. On the surface, some might call this "marketing." I think it's so much more. Because this work is really about stepping into your next evolution. About harnessing the things you never see coming, the ways that life continues to push you to grow, the ways you're called to stay awake in life. This is really about having the courage to pivot and never stop evolving.

Most often, the people I serve are making a pivot in their business too. They never saw it coming, but they have a burning desire to evolve that they just can't ignore.

Like Rachel[3], who wanted to start helping people with hormone health—*not* weight loss like she'd been doing for years. So, she upleveled her messaging to speak to what she really wanted to do and called in clients who were a perfect fit for her brilliance.

Or Tim[3], who wanted to facilitate in-person retreats—*not* online groups like people expected of him. So, he boldly pivoted into this new territory and learned how to use his words and content to appeal to the exact right people. Now, he enjoys traveling the world and connecting with amazing humans in person.

Or Desiree[3], who wanted to close her brick-and-mortar accounting firm and work exclusively with online business owners. Now, she has freedom to work anywhere in the world and helps heart-centered change-makers maximize their business finances for an even greater impact. And a steadily growing audience who easily become clients because her messaging is so laser focused.

---

[3] Names changed to protect privacy

In each case, they made the decision to pivot in their business. To follow the nudge they never saw coming. So, we created silky-smooth messaging and content plans to make this pivot the best thing that ever happened to their heart-centered businesses. Now, they do work that delights and invigorates them. They feel renewed, and their impact keeps growing. They show up boldly and confidently for their dreams and know exactly how to keep attracting the right people who need their messages.

You see, I don't believe it's our destiny to stay stagnant. And sometimes the most unexpected twists, the things you never see coming, are exactly what you need to launch you into *more* of who you were born to be.

But you have to be open to it. Awake to the ways that life is calling you into more. Be brave enough to make changes. Wise enough to know that it's all leading you to exactly where you're supposed to go.

These are just some of the lessons my curly blonde-haired, blue-eyed girl has helped me realize. And we'll continue to learn and grow together, evolving more and more into who we're meant to be and helping other people do the same.

I was meant to be her mom. That I know for sure. She is full of joy and laughter. She reminds me daily that those are the things that matter; the rest are just details.

I was meant to be the business owner I am today. My calendar is full of what brings me joy—the people I work with, the impact they create, the vibration of words and emotions that spark the desire for personal evolution.

The things I never saw coming have ushered me into *more* of who I'm meant to be.

I'm sure your story is different from mine, but the lessons are the same. In business, and in life, magic happens when you stay open to all the things you never knew you needed. The things you never saw coming.

The biggest surprises turn out to be your biggest blessings.

About Ashley

Ashley Fina is a messaging and content coach who has helped hundreds of business owners attract more of the exact right people through their online presence. Her approach to marketing is a blend of manifestation and energy, stand-out messaging, and stellar copywriting to create a simple but profound system for entrepreneurs to grow their businesses.

Ashley has seen how the power and energy of words transforms the lives of not only a business's audience, but the entrepreneur behind the words as well. Realizing that there was a hole in the online marketing world, she knew she had to serve heart-centered business owners who are committed to their bigger mission.

She was bitten by the entrepreneurial bug in 2015 when she started her private practice as a licensed therapist in Pittsburgh, Pa. She enjoyed her therapy practice, with amazing clients and a wait list, until she eventually dove into the world of online entrepreneurship in 2019.

Powerful Synergy

The years of learning how to market for herself, studying copywriting with an insatiable passion, and realizing that messaging for your business is actually about purpose and impact (so much more than just marketing) has landed her where she is today, getting to do work that's soulful, powerful, impactful, and *fun*!

Connect with Ashley

Facebook: https://www.facebook.com/ashley.austin.1257
Instagram: https://www.instagram.com/ashleyfina_/

From Special Education Teacher to Homeschool Mompreneur

Christine Furman

Have you ever felt like you have multiple passions that are pulling you in different directions? This is where I found myself a few years back. I pursued my childhood dream of becoming a teacher and loved every second of it! I was shaping the young minds of our future, teaching kids of all ages and abilities, and instilling valuable life lessons that would serve them for years to come. The students in my classrooms were my children. I loved them like my own and truly wanted the best for them, but my ability to spend hours preparing for my classroom decreased when my own family started to grow. How was I going to fulfill my passion of being an educator when all I wanted to do in the newborn and toddler season was stay home with my children and soak up every precious moment with them?

I quickly realized that my heart was at home, especially during commutes to work and difficult moments in the classroom. One day, after an intruder drill, it hit me so hard: I was preparing young, innocent children for a worst-case scenario that was all-out frightening. Even though it was just a drill, it didn't make the situation any easier. We had to drop what we were doing in an instant and instruct the kids to pick up anything that could be used as a weapon. (What a scary thought—*grab an object you use every day in a room that is supposed to be your safe space away from home and use it as a weapon*!) Not once when I was in college did I imagine I would be preparing myself and my students for a situation like this. It was truly heartbreaking. I had to confirm my students were all accounted for, remain calm, and reassure them that I was there to protect them.

Powerful Synergy

But I couldn't help thinking about my own children, and what I want for them and their future. Did I want them to experience an intruder drill in a classroom? Did I want to spend my precious time away from them every day? I know I had a great schedule as a teacher, but I wanted more time with them. Enough was enough. I needed to figure out a way to stay home with my babies and raise them like I always envisioned I would.

Let's take a moment to jump back to my first year at Robert Morris University, where it all began. I remember walking into a class with a professor who made me think, *I want to be like her when I grow up.* She was confident, vibrant, and full of excitement. She had such a great vibe, and I knew I wanted to take as many classes from her as I could. I would often find myself in her office just to be in her presence. You see, I grew up in the country, and I loved everything about city life and the finer things. When the opportunity came to attend a two-week trip to the inner-city schools of Philadelphia, I was all in! I learned so much about myself as a person: my morals, values, and how not everyone has the same integrity in life. My mission has and will always be to help meet kids where they are, improve their skills, and identify why they don't understand a skill. I learned very quickly that this is not the goal of all educators. I was able to confide in my professor about some unethical things going on that made me uncomfortable—it was eye-opening to say the least, and I grew tremendously as an educator during that time.

My teaching experience ranges from the best-case scenario to challenging at times. After a difficult first year, I realized I was not equipped to be the educator I envisioned myself to be. I needed more knowledge on how to best meet the needs of *all* my students. I decided to go back to school for my master of special education degree. It was the best thing I could have done for myself personally and professionally. I continued to grow and was ready to step into my spiritual gift of being a special education teacher. Of course, there were still challenges, but during my time in the life-skills classroom, I was able to see how I could meet the needs of my students in all capacities. I was also creating a multi-sensory curriculum that would be pivotal to me in my future endeavors as an entrepreneur.

I firmly believe that each of these moments helped to lay the foundation and steps toward my future. Lessons I learned during each challenge pushed me to the next level. I experienced life as a professional: learning how to research and assess skills, talk to educators and parents, discuss action plans to set children up for success, manage a classroom of children all learning at different rates and levels, de-escalate meltdowns, and ensure that children felt loved and safe. I truly enjoyed my time in the classroom and learned so much, but the desire to stay home and experience life with my kids was about to become a reality.

Before taking the leap of faith to stay home, I started dabbling in a few business ideas to prove that I could still earn an income while being home with my kids. The problem was that I was forcing it; the business ideas I came up with were not using my true God-given gifts. Sure, I threw an amazing first birthday party for my daughter, but did that really mean I wanted to become an event planner? I was able to talk to people and connect, but did selling skincare regimens light me up? No way! These options weren't using my strengths and talents as an educator.

Just as I was trying to figure it out and navigate this next chapter in my life, I received a life-changing call. I won a scholarship for an entrepreneur program. It was with none other than the professor who inspired me throughout my college career. It was an opportunity for me to discover my true purpose in life, find a way to stay home with my babies, use my God-given gifts, and create an income and legacy for my family. This opportunity opened my eyes to the fact that I could teach beyond the four walls of the classroom.

Powerful Synergy

Why was I even considering walking away from a full-time teaching position in Pennsylvania, one of the hardest states in which to secure a teaching job? I was giving up full benefits, a decent salary, retirement, and something that I worked so hard for in college. You must think I am crazy; I know some people did. But what I was gaining was so much more! The ability to provide my kids with the best possible education, travel with my husband, and help other moms feel connected, while providing entertainment and education for their children, all while creating time and financial freedom for my family. It was the best of both worlds.

Here is where things became tricky though: I was a teacher, not a business owner. Put me in a room full of kids, and I can find ways to entertain them, but figuring out all the aspects of a business was harder than I realized. This meant 5 a.m. wake ups to tackle tasks before everyone else woke up and give myself some quiet time. I was creating a curriculum while the kids were playing or watching a movie. But one of my favorite parts during this time was recording videos with my kids. I love that I have a vault of educational videos where my kids help to show others how to complete a task, learn their alphabet, or practice math skills. Not every video was full of laughs and smiles, though. Nope. There were definitely moments of tears and tantrums. As *authentic* as it was, it turns out it was actually helpful for my clients. Many noted that it helped them by seeing that my kids weren't perfect, and it allowed them to observe ways that I handled discipline or moments of frustration.

Raising toddlers, running a business, creating curriculum, keeping up with the house, and doing all the things while my husband traveled for work was no easy task. I had moments of doubt, *Why did I start a business*? All I wanted to do was play with my kids and connect with other moms at the park. It could have been very easy to throw in the towel, but I knew deep down God called me to a higher purpose. So, I kept moving forward even on the hard days. I remember putting the kids down for a nap as quickly as possible so I could either get on a call or work during that small window of uninterrupted time. This was a challenging time for sure. I was overstimulated and frustrated because it was so hard to balance it all. But then, the moments of positivity shined through when I saw kids learn and grow right before my eyes. When I connected families who lived in the same neighborhood and didn't even know it, and kids' eyes lit up when they completed activities and crafts at my events. The hugs that I received from them were like no other. I was doing it! I was teaching, connecting families, and spending time with my kids all at the same time. *Finally!*

It has been a blessing to link arms with families and help set them up for a lifetime of success with my programs. Momspiration412® Worldwide was founded to connect families and offer support and guidance for moms on their journeys. What started as in-person meetups in Pittsburgh, Pa., grew to be a worldwide virtual community. Now, I am able to offer resources and encouragement for families globally through the *Educating Kids & Connecting Families* podcast as well as meetups in the Pittsburgh and Augusta, Ga., areas with the plan to expand. My desire to educate continued to show up during our meetups, and the second part of my business, EduPlay® Learning, was developed. I started creating and teaching a hands-on multi-sensory curriculum that meets kids right where they are in a fun and meaningful way!

During 2020, I took all the knowledge and expertise from those in-person events and began to host virtual events for families to have some sort of normalcy during this time of uncertainty. I started offering activity kits for families, allowing them to entertain and educate their kids at home. This was the beginning of something amazing! I was able to provide education to kids in their living rooms with the help and guidance of their parents and me, a certified teacher. I was also able to provide the parents with support and guidance while they navigated this new role. We sang, crafted, cooked, and played games all from the comfort of their homes. This opened EduPlay Learning up to a world of possibilities.

Now the EduPlay Learning Academy helps families get started on their homeschool journey with a customized curriculum that meets them right where they are and sets them up for a lifetime of success, instilling confidence in children and parents alike while creating memories that last a lifetime. I often hear from my clients that they are grateful for the love and support I offer them and their children. Homeschooling can be overwhelming and confusing, but I love that I can be there to help reduce the overwhelm, navigate the journey, and find strategies that work best for each family.

After all the education I have had and experienced, I started seeing the impact I was making all while being home with my kids. I was connecting families through Momspiration412 Worldwide Communities, educating kids with hands-on activities through EduPlay Learning, sharing resources and expert advice on the *Educating Kids and Connecting Families* podcast, and homeschooling my kids through it all. My business continues to pivot and grow but the mission to help set families up for success and educate kids in a fun, meaningful, and individualized way remains. It lights me up to meet families where they are, offering strategies and curriculum to help them balance it all.

Every part of this journey led me to where I am today, and I know this is just the beginning. There are still so many more families to impact and inspire. If you are a mom thinking about running a business to stay home with your children, do it. Of course there will be challenging moments, frustration, and doubt, but the time with your kids will be worth it. If you are thinking about homeschooling but you're concerned about what or how to teach, be sure to check out the *Educating Kids and Connecting Families* podcast for resources and encouragement. Rise above the challenges and rejoice in the moments of triumph. Make the memories, be curious, and see each moment as a chance to *Learn, Create, and Have FUN*!

About Christine

Special education teacher turned homeschool mompreneur with a *huge* vision to revolutionize education and connect families worldwide!

Christine Furman, MEd, is a dedicated wife, homeschool mom, podcast host, and educator with over 20 years of experience in elementary and special education. Teaching is her passion and has led her to provide advice and hands-on education for families around the world! She is the host of the *Educating Kids and Connecting Families* podcast, and her mission is to empower families through encouragement, inspiration, and connection while equipping them to effectively educate their kids in a fun and meaningful way. As the CEO of Educating Kids and Connecting Families and founder of Momspiration412 Worldwide and EduPlay Learning, she has grown a loyal following by being an expert contributor on the radio, various podcasts, TV shows, international stages, magazines, and family-oriented events!

During her time in the classroom, she was able to meet the needs of all learners regardless of their age or ability. Christine created a safe environment that provided an opportunity to learn through educational games, interactive activities, and real-life experiences. These experiences helped her transition from classroom teacher to homeschool mompreneur, which allows her to connect, serve, and educate families worldwide while homeschooling. Momspiration412 Worldwide Communities connect families and offer support and guidance for moms on their journey while the EduPlay Learning curriculum, programs, and academy provide guidance to help families embrace their child's curiosity and learn through interactive activities that develop independence and build confidence.

Connect with Christine

www.christinefurman.com
YouTube - https://www.youtube.com/@eduplaylearning
FB - https://www.facebook.com/groups/educatingkidsconnectingfamilies
EduPlay IG - https://www.instagram.com/eduplaylearning/
Christine IG - https://www.instagram.com/ms.christinefurman/
Email - christine@momspiration412.com

I Do. I Did. I'm Done!
Surviving to Thriving in Motherhood, Divorce, and Entrepreneurship

Melissa Ghelarducci Hancock

Reflecting on my journey from "I do" to "I'm done," I'm struck by the resilience, inspiration, and determination that have carried me through it all. (This isn't what *I* thought, but what others have said to me along the way.) The road from marriage to divorce court was not one I ever anticipated. Still, I navigated it with a fierce purpose that has proven me "brave," according to Kelly Dzana when she interviewed me on KDKA's *Talk Pittsburgh*. As I thought about it, the word resonated with me. Channeling fear, anger, disappointment, sarcasm, spite, and yes ... bravery, transformed into my purpose and driving force! I never dreamt it would help me navigate a path of self-discovery that intersected with motherhood, divorce, finding my tribe, and ultimately, entrepreneurship. I always tell my clients, "Tell me your story," and now I share mine.

I Do: The Beginning of a Tumultuous Journey

My divorce cake said, "I served 20 years to life" (in a marriage, not prison!). Ah, the classic love story: boy meets girl in our local pub. He started his career as a cop. I was a teacher juggling at least four jobs: substitute teaching, cleaning houses, nannying, tutoring, and whatever else I could squeeze in. Two years into our courtship and ... surprise! We were going to be parents. Cue the panic. My initial reaction was to consider an abortion, fearing disapproval from my devout Italian Christian family. To my surprise, they were more understanding than I expected: I found out my brothers were in the same boat before they were married. So, we moved forward with wedding plans and our *I Dos*, blissfully unaware of the storm brewing on the horizon.

Life threw us a curveball early on: our child had ADHD, oppositional defiant disorder, and sensory processing disorder. If you've never walked that path, it's a roller coaster with no seatbelts. Our daughter's endless energy and fierce defiance put immense strain on our relationship. We had in-home services to help us cope with her behavior, but my ex couldn't stand someone else telling us how to raise our child. Despite the challenges, I fought for our daughter's individualized education plan (IEP) to help her in school. I navigated her needs as best I could, often without support from my husband.

Navigating the complex world of special needs parenting requires immense patience, understanding, and a willingness to advocate fiercely for my child. It was a lonely and exhausting journey, one that I often felt I was walking alone. My husband's short temper and reluctance to engage with the necessary support services left me feeling isolated and overwhelmed. I was determined to do whatever it took to ensure our daughter received the care and support she needed though.

I Did: The Struggles and Triumphs of Family Life

I entered this marriage believing we'd be together forever, just like our parents. I understood that marriage was a give-and-take relationship, though it often felt like I was the one giving while he was taking. I worked hard as a service coordinator for the county mental health early intervention unit and later as a developmental specialist in early intervention. My career choices were driven by the need to better understand and support our daughter and our son, who came six years after his sister.

I did everything in my power to be the best mother and wife I could be. From substitute teaching in my kids' school district to advocating for more therapy and support for my daughter, I put my heart and soul into our family. But, the lack of respect and understanding from my husband and my in-laws was demoralizing. They often dismissed my concerns, thinking I was overreacting because of my professional background.

Then, life threw another curveball—a car accident, involving a close friend at the time and fellow police wife, that left me with a broken pelvis, a torn ligament in my knee, and multiple surgeries. I was out of work for two years, and our financial situation became precarious.

My ex's response to my needs, during this time, was initially supportive but turned bitter. I will never forget asking for help with the potty chair, and he said, "You put yourself into that wheelchair; you get yourself out!" The event was a turning point, highlighting the cracks in our marriage and my realization that I deserved better. Later fights involved verbal, mental, and eventually other forms of abuse. The kids saw a lot—especially my daughter, who now suffers from severe anxiety and has a lot of triggers to trauma. To this day, we have patched holes in the walls and cracked doors from him trying to break them down when I was hiding. I leave them there as a reminder of how things were.

The physical pain from the accident was immense, but the emotional pain of feeling abandoned and unsupported was even more overwhelming. It became clear that I needed to take control of my life and make the difficult decision to end a marriage that was no longer healthy or supportive. The journey ahead was daunting, but I knew that staying in an abusive and unhappy relationship was not an option any longer.

I'm Done: Reality Check

Seventeen years and two kids later, I decided it was time to say, "I'm done!" The questions raced through my mind: How could I afford an attorney? What about the house? What about insurance? I had to go on medical assistance for a long time. How would we tell the kids and our families?

Powerful Synergy

My ex had been a good dad and husband at the beginning of our marriage. He worked hard, provided for us, and tried to keep our family happy. But over time, his anger and anxiety from his job and our family life, coupled with a heavy dose of egotism, eroded the foundation of our relationship. I am not perfect either. I have my faults and resentments, but abuse in any form was unacceptable, and while I endured various forms—it was a clear signal that I needed to act.

When you must consider police involvement and you happen to be married to a law enforcement officer, the situation is frightening and embarrassing for all involved. As a trained specialist, I had run through the protocol with my husband to attempt to have him seek help for our family with me. Therapy is only for those who want to change their path. If they choose not to be involved, you can't force them. But he was also very proud, and I still wished to protect our privacy. I decided not to highlight what was really happening in our household back then. However, I offer to you that maybe that was not the best choice for me, my children, or even my husband. I also experienced first-hand the adage that *blood is thicker than water*. I had a great relationship with my in-laws, but they protected him first, before the kids and me. My whole world fell apart, and I had little to no voice.

I am telling you all of this to let you know we have, more or less, made it out on the other side. However, be very careful when selecting a custodial arrangement. It is not just about sharing the kids. It is about ensuring they are in an environment where they shall be given the most positive outlook and the best access to the opposite parent. News flash: if you are being mistreated in your marriage, chances are you will be mistreated in your custody situation too, and that can mean anything from false allegations to unfair statements behind your back when the children are having their custodial time with your former partner.

My decision to leave was not made lightly. It involved countless sleepless nights, tears, and an overwhelming fear and uncertainty about the future. But deep down, I knew that I deserved to live a life free from abuse and negativity and that my children needed a mother who was strong, independent, and capable of providing them with a stable and loving environment.

The process of ending a marriage and breaking free from a toxic relationship was intense, especially doing it alone, especially with an officer. I only had my closest friends and family, well... and my attorney, to help me, and attorneys are not cheap. My case was around fifty thousand dollars and still ensues over custody after almost seven years post-divorce.

Unfortunately, parental alienation is also an issue. This is when one parent manipulates a child to unjustly reject, or fear, the other parent. My heart breaks daily as I fight for a normal relationship with my son, and each time we spend time together, I realize it will take a long time to get there.

Every court date still feels like I am walking into a battlefield armed with nothing but the truth and a glimmer of hope. Despite the affairs, threats, stalking, tire slashing, protection from abuse (PFA) order, and legal battles, I cling to the belief that I am setting an example of resilience and perseverance for my kids. Every setback is a lesson in grit and determination, even if that light at the end of the tunnel sometimes feels like an oncoming train. But deep down, I know that I deserve to live a life free from abuse, and negativity, not fearing for my life and that my children need a mother who is strong, independent, and capable of providing them with a stable and loving environment.

Building a Business from the Ashes: The Birth of Divorce Coach Melissa

In the aftermath of my divorce, I faced a choice: succumb to despair or rise from the ashes with a renewed sense of purpose. I chose the latter. Channeling my inner phoenix, I transformed my pain into a platform for empowerment. Thus, Divorce Coach

Melissa was born. I Do. I Did. I'm Done! became a beacon of hope for others navigating the treacherous waters of divorce.

Whenever I was told I needed to get a *real job* or that I was *crazy*, it fueled my determination to create something meaningful. I envisioned a service that would help others navigate the complexities of divorce, connecting them with the right resources and saving them from costly mistakes. This realization led me to specialize in divorce coaching, focusing on transition, trauma recovery, and co-parenting with a hands-on approach that only someone who has lived through it can provide. We can all thank my ex for creating the new me! (Ha! I never even thought of it till now.)

In 2023, amidst the chaos of the COVID-19 pandemic, I established I Do. I Did. I'm Done! Divorce & Breakup Coaching. Certified and recognized by the Bar Association, I set out to help others transition from surviving to thriving, one layer at a time. I became involved with groups like Pittsburgh's Elevated & Emerging Leaders (PEEL) and Inspired Women South Hills, and I became an ambassador for the South West Regional Chamber of Commerce in Bridgeville, surrounding myself with like-minded, business-oriented, and forward-thinking individuals. I believe, "Your vibe attracts your tribe." This journey opened my eyes to the power of philanthropy and the importance of building a supportive community.

My business quickly gained traction as more and more people sought guidance and support during their divorce and breakup journeys, especially after the pandemic. I can leverage my own experiences and insights to help my clients navigate their challenges, providing them with the tools and strategies needed to move forward with confidence and resilience. It is incredibly rewarding to see the positive impact my work is having—women finding their true voice again, armed with the information they need.

I've been blessed to share my story on shows like *Empowering You,* CBS/KDKA's *Talk Pittsburgh*, and various podcasts. I even started my podcast, *Untying Loves' Knots: Navigating Divorce & Healing Trauma*, to spread the word that no one must go through this alone. My mission is to guide others with the same determination and humor that got me through my journey.

My experiences as a single mother and divorcée provide a unique perspective that resonates deeply with my clients. I built my business on the foundation of empathy, understanding, and the unwavering belief that everyone deserves a chance to rebuild and thrive.

Embracing the New Normal

Creating a new normal for myself and my children involved redefining our family dynamic and forging new traditions. We embraced change, turning our focus toward the future rather than dwelling on the past. Holidays and birthdays became opportunities to create new memories.

Reflecting on my journey from merely surviving to truly thriving, I'm filled with gratitude and humility. Every setback and challenge fueled the fire within me, forging a path from the ashes to a place of strength and empowerment. My journey is a testament to the power of resilience and the transformative potential of pain. I've built a life of purpose and passion from the ashes of a challenging marriage and a tumultuous divorce. My mother always said, "Hang in there; help is on the way," and I never envisioned I would be that help!

About Divorce Coach Melissa

Melissa Ghelarducci Hancock, a proud Pittsburgh "yinzer," knows firsthand the challenges of navigating a divorce while raising children with special needs. As a mother of two kids with ADHD, sensory processing disorder, and oppositional defiance disorder, she brings both personal experience and deep understanding to the table. Melissa has been a dynamic teacher and developmental specialist for over 25 years, working with children with delays and special needs. After her divorce, she also became a certified divorce coach. Drawing from the life lessons and traumatic experiences of being married to a police officer for 20 years, she helps others say I'M DONE and navigate the trauma and overwhelm that the end of a marriage can cause.

As the owner of I Do, I Did. I'm Done! Divorce & Breakup Coaching, she is known as Divorce Coach Melissa, Pittsburgh's #1 Divorce Coach. She specializes in transition, recovery, co-parenting, trauma, and high-conflict situations, particularly working with first responders, medical professionals, and families with special needs children. She combines her expertise in child development with her personal experiences and education to offer compassionate, no-bullshit, and practical advice to those navigating the complexities of divorce.

Melissa's podcast, *Untying Loves' Knots: Navigating Divorce & Healing Trauma*, allows her guests to share their stories of divorce, co-parenting, abuse, trauma, and overcoming it all with grace and a bad-ass attitude. She has been featured on CBS/KDKA *Talk Pittsburgh*, talking all things divorce and beyond. She is currently developing divorce recovery classes and building divorce support groups both locally and online.

Connect with Melissa

I DO. I DID. I'M DONE! Divorce & Breakup Coaching
www.divorcecoachmelissa.com
Facebook: https://www.facebook.com/divorcecoachmelissa
Email: divorcecoachinabox@gmail.com
Untying Loves' Knots: The Podcast www.untyinglovesknots.com
Facebook: @untyinglovesknots
Email: untyingknotstm@gmail.com

Recovering from American Dream Burnout

Diane Greco Allen

I had it all! I was a nurse married to a surgeon, had four children close in age, ultimately moved to a four bedroom Tudor home (that required updating), drove autos that many dream of owning, had a co-membership to the local country club, indulged in shopping sprees, decorations, and vacations to fine resorts. We raised multiple pets including rabbits and a tarantula. It appeared I was living the American Dream, not outrageous, but a very comfortable lifestyle. What was happening behind the scenes told a different story.

The truth is, doctors and nurses can be a tough crowd to hang with—with or without compassion —we are wired fixers and can be intimidating in most cases. We both had a great work ethic, but this lifestyle was slowly killing me.

Being a stay-at-home mother for almost 25 years taught me some valuable lessons about balance. As I tried to keep up with the demands of motherhood, chores, paperwork, planning, and travel, my children witnessed my chronic health decline, and it impacted their younger years. I was either a nonstop woman always on the go, go, go, or I was on the floor (literally passing out) from sheer exhaustion! I had to make some really tough decisions to change my life.

Looking back, instead of adding in time for self-care, I took on more caregiving roles with agencies and the family that spread me thin. I was emotionally volatile and depleted. I cried at the drop of a hat.

I had attempted to finish school during my pregnancies, but it didn't work out. My nursing license lapsed after my fourth child was born, as I embraced being a stay at home mother, wife, family coordinator, caregiver, and designated driver.

While raising my children and staying actively engaged in their school, sports, and extracurricular activities, I felt obligated to visit extended family on weekends. I had accepted that my nursing career was being placed on the back burner, after only seven years of experience. I did not have full control of my life and energies.

Timeline Awareness: Making Sense of Our Past Experiences to Heal

One of my many specialists over the years led me to a doctor of functional medicine. This inspired me to learn more. I began taking classes and was certified through a Lifestyle Balance Program offered at the University of Pittsburgh and then the Functional Medicine Coaching Academy (https://functionalmedicinecoaching.org/).

While on my roller coaster health journey, not fully healed, I was introduced to the timeline assessment tool via my coaching course with the Functional Medicine Coaching Academy. It was instrumental in helping me map out the history of my life events to learn about myself and what occurrences lined up with or led to unwellness. This, and many other tools, allow me to assist others to do the same. Reviewing a timeline of past experiences can help connect the dots around physical and emotional precursors, exposures, learned habits, and environmental factors that impact our health and wellbeing.

Growing up, our house was a bit chaotic and disorganized with my dad's upholstery business on our family property, and the need for my mom to work. Sleepless nights began early in my life, sharing a bedroom with my sister who was born when I was ten and constantly cried from colic. I became a second mother, assisting with chores and her care, while my mother worked two jobs. Looking back, we all dealt with some learning challenges. I was the fourth of six children: four boys and two

Diane Greco Allen

girls. Heavily influenced by our Italian Catholic upbringing and my mom's work connection to PONY baseball, we attracted similar families who became our extended family.

During my childhood, I had a paper route, assisted with cleaning and painting rental properties, babysat, did home chores, and worked summers at both fast and upscale food venues. Our Sunday routine started at 5 a.m. to deliver the morning paper. Then, after mass and our pasta dinner ritual, we were motivated to go for leisurely drives with promises of ice cream. My dad was my connection to ice cream, peanuts, and popcorn. My mom was my connection to cooking and baking sweets, bread, pasta, and pizza. I learned this from reflecting on my food relationships. Like most Italian moms, her boundaries around feeding guests were nonexistent.

Family and food were always threads throughout my life. I developed weight challenges early during my childhood, and I never forgot the first time I was called "fat" by an adult. (We often don't realize how these tags about body image affect us.)

Cooking and preparing food became second nature. As a young girl, I became the family cook and enjoyed solitude in the kitchen. In high school, though, I sort of broke out of my "shell" and became more outgoing: a disco dancer, and the Forrest Gump of the town, walking for miles a day. I was always paying attention to my body image so I wouldn't be that "fat little Italian girl" anymore. I had developed the ultimate sweet tooth, but I thought balancing it with a salad and proteins would make a difference. I had no issue substituting a meal with leftover homemade pizza, pasta, ice cream, and peanut butter smoothies, cake, pie, or Italian cookies. These treats supported my "carboholic" tendencies.

After high school, I pursued a career in nursing. I saw this as my chance to help others with my inherent empathy, which ran in the family.

After graduation in 1982, I immediately joined the staff at Mercy Hospital in Pittsburgh. Nursing school and clinical work

69

was rigorous and stressful, but I didn't mind working double shifts for extra money. My *healthy* obsession with taking the steps in the hospital, power walking, gym-rat routines, and traveling adventures, but they were also connected to the unhealthy trappings of vending machines, convenience foods, and unhealthy cafeteria offerings. My high-carb diet fueled my high energy spurts. Stress and emotional eating caused frequent dental visits for tooth decay and multiple root canals, as well as doctor's visits for endoscopies, migraines, irregular painful menstrual periods (with horrible PMS), urinary tract infections (UTIs), and irritable bowel syndrome (IBS). Overextending myself and leaning into sweets, quick carbs, and comfort foods when I wanted to feel good was finally catching up with me.

I was flexible and often rotated throughout the various hospital units, finally advancing to the cardiovascular surgical intensive care unit, which taught me more about how the body responds in an acute surgical setting from unhealthy living. After six years of clinical practice at Mercy Hospital in Pittsburgh, I relocated to Philadelphia to be with my partner, who I married a year later. That was the beginning of a new relationship with new environments, street foods, and all Philadelphia had to offer for foodies like us.

Overwhelm Defines Me

While working 12-hour shifts and just after moving and starting my position at Thomas Jefferson University Hospital in Philadelphia, I experienced fertility issues related to an area of concern during a pap smear, but within a year (without intervention), surprisingly we had our first child. Consequently, my nursing career was placed on the back burner during maternity leave. When a job opportunity opened in Pittsburgh for my husband, we relocated back and had three additional children within five years, all delivered by C-section. I attempted to go back to work but our family grew so quickly it seemed counterintuitive.

Diane Greco Allen

I became a "golfer's widow" most weekends and didn't embrace the country club lifestyle as much as my husband, so I frequently called on family troops and hired help for support. Our four children's health issues throughout childhood and into their college years led us to pediatrician offices and ERs with allergies and inhalers, anaphylaxis, an acute case of mononucleosis, and other acute scenarios as well as broken bones and a near loss of an eye. That last one especially heightened my awareness around my children's safety.

As I taxied my kids and their friends to school activities and events, fast food was our crutch, and my children bonded with these unhealthy food memories. Many mornings we ate bagels for a quick breakfast, and as the Happy Meal toy bin grew, so did my exhaustion. I went from being a *house manager*, family historian, homeroom mom, intense scout mom, and "mom's taxi" to dealing with frequent illnesses, naps, and tardiness.

Even our dinners at home were stressful, frequently interrupted by phone calls while my husband was on call. His beeper caused anxiety for the whole family. The negative energy was palpable.

Intertwined with my children's health and learning challenges were frequent ER and doctor's office visits for me. As a patient, I grew frustrated with unanswered questions from specialists. Unable to perform tasks as a distracted and fatigued wife and mother led to chronic feelings of inadequacy. Migraines, pain, and chronic fatigue became the norm. Even with my nurse training running through my mind, I failed to nurse myself. I thought my only hope was medicine, chiropractors, and additional surgeries, as I sought an answer to what ailed me. I also reached out to a licensed counselor, Al-Anon, NAMI, and other groups to assist me as a co-dependent of family substance abuse.

By the time we got our children through college, my memory was failing, my body was in total burnout, and I was giving up hope: feeling wiped out, weak, and in a wheelchair twice dealing with near adrenal shutdown. I was literally preparing for my death. My weight maxed out at 189 pounds. Then, I ended up dropping 60 pounds while in severe pain and unable to eat. In desperation, I requested hospice, adamant they had missed something. Next, I sought out several experts in endocrinology. After hundreds of tests, trials with multiple types of medications, outpatient procedures, several surgical interventions, and dental extractions—like a strike of lightning—I looked in the mirror and said, "None of this is working, there has to be a better way!"

I was no longer going to be a conformist to the conventional sick ideology. I later learned that postpartum fatigue, gut microbiome, hormone imbalances, and black mold exposure were a part of my hypothyroidism (similar to Hashimoto's thyroiditis) and immune suppression, along with a physically and emotionally toxic environment.

Taking the First Step

Stepping up to the "plate" in a different way literally and figuratively took courage, discipline, and mindful eating awareness. Instead of chasing hormones, I was chasing natural nutrition experts. Over 20 years, I engaged in programs and research around healing using natural alternative modalities regarding holistic wellness. Like the song, "The Sound of Silence" by Simon and Garfunkel, I began to listen to my body and learn about myself and the habits I had formed. Assistance with healing myself while at the same time reflecting on my life was a process. I was ready to address my causes of burnout as a pleaser and had to learn to disengage and not have unrealistic expectations about others or myself.

Now, It was time to build and practice boundaries!

Purposeful Investment with Boundaries

As I prioritized and clarified my needs, my relationships changed. I jumped off the medical merry-go-round and jumped on board with mindful practitioners who understood the value of nutrition-based sciences; addressing trauma, injury, and grief; and the healing process around gut health. My gut was a disaster.

Unfortunately, my marriage broke down in the attempt to heal from the lack of family boundaries.

Food and eating patterns were key aspects of emotional healing. I *knew* my kids by their food memories, and they knew me in the same way. Time was my ally, though, and food became the way to bring my family together and heal in a more balanced way. Health, wellness, and life balance through holistic approaches brought forth our ability to digest food and experience life differently.

Functional Medicine Coaching Academy

My training and certification with the Functional Medicine Coaching Academy (FMCA), a unique partnership with the Institute for Functional Medicine (IFM), was a purposeful investment. I was stepping into the field of functional medicine, which addresses the root causes of disease and promotes wellness by focusing on the whole person, while addressing overall immune and digestive wellness.

I wanted to help people heal, so using functional nutrition principles and the skills I developed, I now guide clients through their health journeys. I help them connect the dots between their past experiences, environmental factors, and their current health issues. I empower them to make sustainable changes in their diets and lifestyles.

Understanding the importance of boundaries, both personal and professional, has been crucial in my journey. Establishing these boundaries has allowed me to maintain my health and well-being while effectively supporting my clients.

Embracing the Functional Nutrition Lifestyle

Living the functional nutrition lifestyle is not just about what you eat; it's about how you live. It's about mindfulness, stress management, and creating a balanced life. I've learned to listen to my body, to understand its needs, and to nourish it properly. This journey has not only transformed my health but has also inspired me to help others find their path to wellness.

My journey from a nursing career to functional nutrition counseling has been a transformative experience. It has taught me the power of food as medicine and the importance of a holistic approach to health. Through functional nutrition, I have found a new purpose and a way to help others achieve optimal health and well-being.

About Diane

Diane Greco Allen, FMCHC, CFNC, is a highly sought after natural functional nutrition counselor and health coach, former critical care nurse, Mindful Eating facilitator, owner of Digestive

Distress Solutions LLC, and proud author of *It Might Be Your Pancreas: Pancreatitis Awareness and Natural Digestive Recovery Edition*. Diane's primary focus is in pancreatic health, which encompasses individuals dealing with pancreatitis, digestive issues, caregiver burnout, supermom syndrome, binge eating with depression and anxiety, and more. She provides cooking, coaching and speaking sessions both virtually and in person to individuals, families, or groups.

As a certified functional nutrition counselor, Diane works with clients to determine the roots of their digestive issues. As a coach, Diane advocates for a healthy holistic lifestyle, balanced nutrition, and overall well-being. She emphasizes the dysfunctional relationship we may have developed with food to encourage positive healthy eating habits. Diane's book, *It Might Be Your Pancreas*, expands on her personal experiences and coaching in prevention and management of pancreatitis and other digestive disorders to nurse and heal your digestive system back to a more functional place. Diane confronts the struggle of eating healthy by emphasizing nutritious meals in a (more tasteful) delicious way. She loves to support others in taking the driver's seat in achieving their health and wellness goals and helps her clients achieve the best possible outcome on their journey to feeling, living, and functioning optimally (being at their best).

Connect with Diane

www.digestivedistresssolutions.com
Email at d.grecoallen@gmail.com
Linktr.ee/dianegrecoallen to purchase my book, *It Might Be Your Pancreas* to learn more about working with me or just see what's cooking!

My Journey to Creating Freedom and Being Present in Business and Family

Priscilla Green

I wanted to be my own boss—a common sentiment for a lot of women—and the motivations for that can vary. But, in my experience, conversations I've had usually center around family needs or obligations.

My motivation was no different. I always wanted to be a mom that was fully present for her kids. But I also wanted to contribute to our family income.

I was able to work part-time in the early years of motherhood, still able to go to the park, take my two kids on fun adventures, and watch them grow. But, as our family grew, so did the need to work full-time. That meant less time with my kids and being unable to attend their school activities and sports. It crushed my heart, and I knew that my kids also felt that change.

Previously, I was that mom who was at every single school event, on the PTO board, and on every field trip ... and then I wasn't.

As my family expenses increased, I needed to contribute more to our household income and found a full-time job at a local company. At this time, my youngest was only a toddler. My first day on the job was actually his second birthday, and it broke my heart to not be with him all day to celebrate this milestone. When he was in preschool, I was working and missed out on all the preschool events and field trips. I also missed holiday shops, field trips, and events for my older two. A very stark contrast to what it was like prior to working full-time.

I was sitting at work one day when my daughter messaged me to ask if I was going to be at her track meet. My heart sank and the feelings of guilt rushed in as I hated to type the words "I'm sorry, but I can't. I'm at work." That was it. My desire to be there for my kids outweighed the desire to sit at a desk in an office that kept me from being at the events and activities, supporting and cheering on my kids.

Not long ago a memory popped up on my Facebook memories feed, and it was a good reminder of how far I have come since working full-time and not having the full freedom to be present for my kids. It read: "I was so lucky to be able to spend the afternoon with Lincoln's class for World Record Day! It isn't often that I get to go to his school events during the day, so I had so much fun."

Getting photos of my kids at their sports or school activities from other moms or friends was a painful reminder of my absence when it mattered. It was so kind of them to share with me, but I couldn't help but think of how that felt for my kids. I felt guilty because I should have been the one there taking the photos.

My son went to division finals in the high jump event for track and field and placed third, which meant he would advance to the Pennsylvania state finals. I wasn't there because I had to work. Even to this day, I still feel the sting of guilt from that image posted on Facebook. It is engraved in my mind and on my heart. I should have been there.

I couldn't help but think how my absence would affect my kids in the long-term. There were comments from my kids about how I was only at a few of their events or activities and the sting of them was a catalyst for me. I didn't want to miss another moment. My determination to build a business life that allowed me the freedom to choose what I could go to and when had grown to a point where I knew that it would become my reality.

The line in the sand was drawn, and I was going to do this!

As I started to see women who were entrepreneurs and business owners online and on social media, I thought about how much that could change my life and the way that I show up as a mom. They were available to their kids and families on their own schedule.

I had tried so many other ways to make money at home over the years prior to working full-time. I tried four different companies that advertised that I could work from home and be successful, and I had some success, but none that would allow me to quit my job. So, the feeling of prior defeat was in the back of my mind.

I was determined to make this work. I had been researching ways to start a business, and using the knowledge and skills that I already had, I decided to start my own virtual assistance business. I decided that I wanted to work with women in my business. I wanted to help other ladies be present for their children while also fulfilling their dreams and goals for themselves and their families. So, I set forth on a journey that would take me on a roller coaster of emotions,

As I was starting out in my business, I saw some changes in my family and my clients. I began to feel at ease and calmer because I could envision where I was heading, and that included being more present and more supportive of my kids' needs. As a *right hand* to business owners, I was able to help other women be present for their own children too. It was such a full-circle moment to support women business owners to fulfill a common goal. My clients have been able to take family vacations and spend time with their children and families, inspiring me to set up my business to allow for the same in my own life.

I started my business when my kids were 17, 16, and nine years old. So, our family was at a point in life that was rapidly changing. We were preparing for college, competing in high school athletics, and seeing the landscape of life moving in a different direction.

My role was changing. I was no longer kissing boo-boos, pushing kids on the swings, or chauffeuring kids to and from sports. I was moving into a new stage of motherhood that included more adult things, like guidance for the next stage of life, college safety, and life-changing decision-making. I clung to each and every moment with the kids. I realized that, soon, my kids would be off to college, and time with them was fleeting. My business allowed me the freedom to support my kids in ways that I would not have been able to if I were still working full-time as an employee.

I built my business in a way that allowed me to be present for my kids and to attend track meets, school activities, and lunches with my mom and to help take care of my dad when he was dealing with health issues. When my son needed surgery, I didn't have to request time off and hope that it was approved. I was able to be there for every single second of his recovery in a way that I couldn't have in my prior job setting. I was able to volunteer during football training season for my son because I now had the freedom to do so. My kids noticed that I was able to be there more. I was again able to support them in a way that I couldn't before starting my business. That ache to be there was no longer a part of my life. I felt a freedom that I had been craving for years as a mom.

My business has helped my family go on vacation and stay in a beachfront condo. I was able to watch them in the ocean and on the beach with a smile on my face and gratitude in my heart. Seeing their smiles and hearing their laughter fed my soul. It is exactly why I do what I do: to be present and make lifelong memories with my family.

My children were a large part of my motivation to create a successful business. I had the drive to show them what is possible in life—that their mom could go from that person that they saw at home, always stressed and feeling guilty, to becoming a leader and an expert in my field. I was showing up for myself and my family in ways that I had never done before. I wanted them to see me succeed and show them the determination and perseverance that I had because I started a business. It also allowed me to show my kids that there are other ways of building your dreams and seeing hard work pay off for your life and family. Yes, they were going to college and had their own goals and their own direction, but I think it's important for children to see that there are other ways to succeed and that the traditional way doesn't work for everyone.

Having the freedom in my business to set my own schedule and choose to work and serve other women has been paramount to my success. I feel good about what I do. I enjoy the relationships that I've built with other women in business. I've been able to celebrate with, encourage, listen to, and learn about their journeys in motherhood and business. My choice to build my business in a way that allows me to share in these moments with my clients is almost as special as my decision to change the trajectory of my own journey and motherhood through my business.

As an online business manager for my clients, I help them free up several hours a week so they can spend time on what matters most to them. Typically, that means their family and their kids ... and I had the same goal in my own business.

I recently took a family vacation to Disney World in Florida. It was a first for not only my kids, but for my husband and me too! Growing up, I always felt like going to Disney was just a dream, so I was very proud to be able to plan and make that dream come true. It would not have been possible without the time and energy that I poured into building my business in a way that allowed *me* the same freedom I help my clients to experience. This trip was an opportunity to make lifelong family memories as the kids are getting older and soon will be flying the coop to go on their own adventures.

Being an accredited online business manager and agency owner gives me the freedom to focus on what truly matters in life. I want the same for every woman who feels the pain in her heart from not having that freedom whether she is a seasoned entrepreneur who feels the burn from trying to do it all or a new entrepreneur desiring to build a successful business as a virtual assistant.

About Priscilla

Priscilla is a distinguished entrepreneur, author, and leader celebrated for her commitment to empowering women-owned businesses to achieve their definition of success. As the founder and CEO of Freedom to Focus Business Support LLC, Priscilla heads an agency known for providing exceptional executive assistance services. Her expertise has been pivotal in helping six-, seven-, and eight-figure enterprises streamline their operations and unlock their full potential.

With over a decade of experience, Priscilla excels in delivering high-level services tailored to the unique needs of business owners. She is passionate about fostering meaningful relationships and developing strategic business solutions, earning her a reputation for offering white-glove services that enable women entrepreneurs to scale their ventures effortlessly.

Beyond her professional achievements, Priscilla finds inspiration in her personal life as a wife and mother of three. She enjoys running, hiking, spending time outdoors, and traveling. Priscilla's family life fuels her dedication to helping other women business owners achieve a harmonious balance between professional success and personal fulfillment.

Connect with Priscilla

Discover how Priscilla can help you reclaim your time and elevate your business by visiting www.freedomtofocusbusinesssupport.net.
Facebook: www.facebook.com/FreedomtoFocus
Instagram: www.instagram.com/freedomtofocus

Loving Mondays

Erika Maddamma

Being an organized, tenacious overachiever had always served me, until I became a mom.

In high school, I would assist the music teacher before class started. All day long I'd go from class to class, raising my hand and offering to help others who were stuck, regardless of the subject. I'd go from seventh period straight to soccer practice. On Thursdays, I used to take a freezing shower in the disgusting girl's locker room and trade my shorts for my poodle skirt to work at the '50s diner nearby. After work, I'd count my tips and then responsibly do my homework in my upstairs bedroom. My days were packed. I liked to do it all, even then.

A decade later, I had my first baby and everything was turned on its head.

I was in the prime of my corporate career. I'd been in sales at a baby car seat and stroller manufacturing company for the past seven years. I loved my job and was finally in my dream role: running big meetings, being the best employee. I had it all.

And I just had my first baby: Kaleb Thomas was my dream come true.

He was pure perfection in every way. I was simply obsessed. Every smile. Every laugh. Every little movement. Every cute outfit change. He fulfilled me in such a profound way.

But dream job + dream baby = so confused

I was paying a *ton* of money for daycare to never see the baby that I had wanted so badly.

It was killing me. Dropping him off before my 8 a.m. start time and picking him up in the evening, only for him to have a quick nap, dinner, bath, and then going to bed. It was not the way I wanted to be a mom. I looked around at everyone else who was doing the same grind. I thought this must be what it was like to be a working mom. I never thought I wanted to be a stay-at-home mom, but how long could I keep going, trying to be my best for everyone? I was being spread too thin. I knew if I wanted things to change, I had to take matters into my own hands. There was no way this was as good as it got.

I also wasn't showing up as my A-student self as an employee. I was cutting hours short so I could spend more time with my son. I would complain every time I had to travel. I cringed at my phone as my boss's face flashed across the screen. I showed up every day with animosity toward the job I once loved but was now robbing me of time with the child I loved way more.

I knew it was time for a change.

Becoming an entrepreneur had been my lifelong dream. In college, I wrote the exact professional organizer business plan I use now.

Actually, I had tried twice before to start this business. But it took having Kaleb to push me to go for it. Yet, the risks had never been higher.

How could I walk away from a great salary? A career I built for myself? That matching 401(k)? And, duh, free baby car seats and strollers—those things are expensive!! How could I let all that go when I had a mortgage and a baby to take care of? Was this the time to take a risk?

So, I learned to love my corporate job again ... for a bit.

Thanks to a group life coaching program, I learned how to manage my thoughts and feel differently toward the same exact job. And my intimidating boss.

It was amazing.

I even figured out how to have more time with my baby. I negotiated working four, 10-hour days and having Fridays off with my son! However, if you've ever worked in corporate, you know respecting boundaries is just *not* a thing, and I wasn't great at holding others accountable to them.

Erika Maddamma

I can clearly remember running to my neighbor's house one Friday in complete tears, seeing if she could watch my son for a little bit because I had to take a 3-hour call and the deadline wouldn't allow for it to wait until Monday. I was devastated. Imagine how I showed up to that meeting—I wasn't doing anyone any favors.

So, even with a whole dedicated Kaleb day, I wasn't fulfilled. I wanted a bigger change. I wanted more time with my baby, and my corporate job wasn't going to give me that.

I hired the same coach I worked with in the group program, but this time one-on-one. I told her my goal was to quit my job. This is it, I thought. I have a plan. I knew what I wanted my business to be. I knew how I wanted to make money.

It was fall of 2019. In December, I would turn 30. A new decade for me and a new decade for the world—2020—what possibilities there would be!

I had never felt more inspired. Leaving my 20s behind. Having a one-year-old. This was the time. I was frickin' determined. I spent time figuring out my offer. How I would run my business. What my numbers had to be to quit my job.

I had a lot of tearful conversations with my husband about this change and I wasn't taking no for an answer. I had a vision and a belief that it would work out, but it was hard for him to see that. He needed proof. I would deliver it to him.

My first paying client was a college student needing to get back to Canada before the borders closed due to COVID-19. I helped her pack her dorm room, unsure if I should actually be out in public at the time. What kind of risk was I taking? So many unknowns. Should I wear a mask? Such a confusing time.

Of course, daycare shut down, so my now 15-month-old baby, who I wanted to spend so much time with, was home. Awesome! But my workload didn't stop and neither did my husband's.

I'd get up at 4 a.m. to get my corporate work done and dig into my business during nap times. We'd alternate who would take their work Zoom calls from the playroom and which calls were *more* important to be taken from our makeshift, home-office spaces.

I was determined to stay present in my corporate job while also building my business. I knew in my heart that I would be an incredible professional organizer even though I didn't have proof yet. But I had belief. And that was all I ever needed.

As things began to open up again, clients started to flow in. Who didn't need organizing then more than ever? Stuck home. No school. No daycare. No office. Everyone had set up dining room offices and classrooms in various parts of their home. What an opportunity!

I would take paid time off (PTO), venturing out during the day and organizing for people. I needed to prove that I could make money organizing people's stuff. I would not fail.

Finally, the day arrived. I was ready to kiss my eight-year corporate life goodbye and forfeit my steady salary and employee benefits. I was going out on my own. I remember calling our VP of sales to let her know I was resigning. I was at my parents' house. It was hot and I was outside by their in-ground pool pacing, unable to sit down. The bottoms of my bare feet hot on the concrete. My hands and my voice were shaking. I was afraid of disappointing her and my team and feared jumping into the unknown. I had a whole spiel thanking the company for all they'd done for me over the years, but it was time for me to spend time with my son. I ended up staying on for three more months, executing a big meeting I was leading, leaving on very good terms.

September 18, 2020, was my last day of work in the corporate world. It's an anniversary I celebrate every year. I had proven to myself I could make the money I needed to pay our bills in my three-day work week. I decided that would give me the balance I needed to contribute to our household and be available to my son.

Although this was such a huge achievement, it was only the beginning.

In 2021, I happily found myself pregnant for the second time. Though overjoyed to grow our family, I knew I needed help running my business. While Kaleb gets the credit for pushing me to get the company off the ground, Jaxson gets credit for building my team.

I maintained my three-day-a-week schedule, balancing my days off entertaining Kaleb with trips to the zoo, parks, and the "jumpy place." I learned I am a more present mom when we get out of the house on little adventures.

But I was constantly feeling pulled. Anxious to get the next paying client. Running to my phone every time it would ding with the potential of a new lead. Frantically responding to the latest inquiry. The drive to earn was pulling me away from my presence with Kaleb. And hadn't spending more time with him been the point?

Knowing I wasn't staying true to my boundaries and with baby number two on the way, I decided to hire assistant organizers to help me with bigger jobs. Slowly, I built trust and confidence to allow them to be on jobs without me. My vision of earning money while not working was starting to come to light.

As my belly grew bigger, so did our profits. We netted over one hundred thousand dollars in sales in 2021, and I relinquished control of the day-to-day of my business to my top assistant, allowing me to completely disconnect and take an eight-week, paid maternity leave.

To this day, I still maintain my Tuesdays and Fridays off. I no longer am pulled to answer every buzz of my phone. In fact, I've removed all notifications. My best clients will wait for my response during my next business hour. I've lost the frantic energy and have fully leaned into the belief that the clients are coming, and the money is flowing.

My days with my clients are fulfilling. I know I am helping them and impacting their lives in a major way. I remember our

Powerful Synergy

first whole house transformation for a client: attic, three bedrooms, main level living spaces, and finished basement. Years of good intentions and lack of time led to a lot of excess stuff. Spring-boarded by our work, our client continues to maintain an organized home. She'll text me when she reorganizes a space, so proud of herself and the personal transformation she has had.

That is why I truly started my business: to impact lives, to show up to a job that isn't work. I fully believe that you should absolutely love what you do. Our time here is short, and we should find joy in the everyday. I tell my boys, now five and two, this as I drop them off at daycare, "Mommy gets to go help another mommy today. I *get* to go to work!"

I love my days with my boys at home. While some days I feel more like a referee, I wouldn't trade these long days, yet short years, for anything. I am proud of myself for setting and holding my boundaries to allow myself this freedom.

I love my journey and I love my story. I wouldn't change one part of it. I wouldn't change the struggles. I wouldn't change the tears. I'm thankful for every misstep because it provided a learning opportunity.

My last business coach encouraged us to "collect fails." So, I set lofty goals. When I don't reach them the first time, I assess why and try again. I learn as I go. My determination and unwavering belief in myself and what I can offer the world has led to my success. I know this is just the tip of the iceberg. Even four years into business, the doubt creeps back in. I have to go back and reaffirm why I started, why I help people in this way, and why I am the best person for the job. The mind is so powerful, yet incredibly simple. Once we have this awareness, the control is there.

If you have a dream, follow it. Push aside those doubts. Write down all the reasons *why* you should do this. Bolster your belief in yourself. That's all you need to have massive success.

Create a life where you love your Mondays as much as your Fridays.

About Erika

Erika Maddamma is a mompreneuer and professional organizer who is full of light and positive energy, inspiring others to live brighter. Her passion for organization has been a lifelong endeavor, starting from a young age and evolving into a fulfilling career. She started Sunny Spaces Organizing in 2020. Erika's meticulous attention to detail and creative organizing solutions have helped hundreds of families transform their spaces and lives.

When she's not bringing order to chaos, Erika enjoys spending quality time with her husband, Nick, and their two energetic boys, Kaleb (five) and Jaxson (two). Whether exploring the outdoors, traveling home to Connecticut, or simply enjoying family moments, she balances her professional and personal life with enthusiasm. Erika is a New England native who now calls Pittsburgh home.

Erika has been featured on Pittsburgh's KDKA and won the 2023 Outstanding Business Leader Award from MEDIA – The Creative Agency.

Connect with Erika

Instagram: Sunny Spaces (@sunnyspacesorganizing)
Facebook: https://www.facebook.com/sunnyspacesorganizing
Please follow us on Instagram and Facebook for more inspiration and organization and decluttering tips: @Sunnyspacesorganzing

A Season for Every Purpose

Theresa Ream

The foundation of greatness starts with being authentic and real in all relationships but most of all with ourselves.

Dear Reader,

My guess is that you are reading this book because you are a mom in business or a mom aspiring to be in business. Whatever the case, keep reading because I will share some great tips and insights. Why am I an expert? Because I have experienced the beautiful and the ugly—the lows and the highs—and have been through many experiences, solved many problems, and put out many fires. My expertise comes from 43 years of running successful multimillion dollar small businesses. For 38 of those years, I was raising two children, and at the age of 62, my husband and I had the privilege of taking on raising our six-year-old grandson, Cash, after he tragically lost his mom to cancer. He is now a happy and healthy 13-year-old and has consistently been a straight-A student since kindergarten.

I have been married to my husband Terry for 46 years, and we have been together since I was 16. The best thing about being with someone since I was a kid is that I can still be a kid with that person—and I take full advantage of that.

What's holding us back?

What holds most women back from having successful businesses while being loving and attentive moms, having healthy relationships with those we care about, and engaging in the self-care we not only deserve but is a must for living the life we desire? For most of us, it's overwhelm, exhaustion, lack of self-direction or lack of control of our schedules, and doing too much.

What's going on?

Bottom line ... women are expected to do more (of everything)!

We run businesses and do the bulk of raising the children. We are responsible for over ninety percent of household chores—usually we take care of the finances and keep an eye on the temperature of the family by making sure everyone is healthy and happy.

Women spend more time preparing for vacations than men and our bedtime routine is up to six times longer than a man's as we shut down the home before bed. We are more involved in our children's schedules, including taking care of their pets (that *they* promised to care for).

There seems to have been a drop in adult leisure time over the last few decades and more family time than in the 1960s. Our parents and grandparents had cocktail dinners at friend's houses, bridge parties, adult-only hobbies, and adult vacations. With fewer adult activities we have less husband-and-wife time and more entertaining the children.

We are more scattered and fragmented than we admit to and it's *not sustainable.*

Phrases like *time-crunch, frantic pace, hectic,* and *whirlwind schedules* are normal life descriptions now. Have you ever felt like you were running a race in scuba flippers?

There is a beautiful quote by Jewel from her book, *Never Broken: Songs Are Only Half the Story*. It goes like this: "Hard wood grows slowly. Be thoughtful about the shape you want it to grow into and be mindful that there is no shortcut to strength and character. Have the patience to allow yourself and your goals to develop."[4]

How do we begin? Let's get into these tactical solutions to remedy overwhelm and exhaustion that many entrepreneurial moms face:

- Guarding our time
- Doing less while increasing quality and productivity
- Having a strategic calendar
- Recognizing the seasons of our lives and going with the flow

You Must Guard Your Time

Interruptions

We are expected to welcome interruptions, but they kill our thinking and creative time. Consider doing your creative work in a place where you won't be interrupted. Now, turn your phone off or at least put it on silent. Some places to get away to are coffee shops, bookstores, libraries, park benches, and beautiful outdoor venues. While at home or in the office, train others that, when you shut your door, there are no interruptions unless someone's arm is falling off.

Some savvy mompreneurs set up a calendar app for open-door office hours (while working at home) just so there are set times for interruptions, questions, and meetings. Avoid asking others to send you emails because many times a quick phone call can take care of so many details and clarifications without filling up your inbox.

Mark Zuckerberg, the cofounder of Facebook and Meta Platforms, sets strict guidelines for his meetings. He requires

---

[4] Quote by Jewel: "Hard wood grows slowly. Be thoughtful about the…" (goodreads.com)

the person requesting the meeting to do their homework and research, so they already have solutions and a plan when they meet with him. This way, people don't come and dump on him without first putting thought and work into what they are bringing him.

Focus Is the Fuel of Creativity

The greatest amount of energy used by a car is when it is starting and gaining speed or when constantly stopping and starting. This holds true for you too. Your mind will be clearer, and your output will be of a much higher quality when you stay focused.

Increased Timelines Equal Increased Quality

Your higher quality work will make you more valuable in the marketplace, earning you more money.

As an ambitious entrepreneur, you will underestimate the time required for the mental activity it takes to complete a project and you will end up planning for the best-case scenario. If your deadlines are too short, you will rush and not turn out high-quality work. Guard your time, and it will have a trickle-down effect on your energetic output.

Do Less

Drastically downsize your daily task list and the number of active goals and have a list of feeder goals waiting.

Would you love to toss stress and hurry out the door and do less while producing higher quality work, earning more, and being a better mother, family member, and friend?

Too many projects and tasks mean less creativity and slower production. Coach and speaker Tony Robbins says, "Most people overestimate what they can do in a year. And they underestimate what they can do in a decade, or two, or three..."5 Our society isn't big on the importance of patience and long-term thinking. There is transformative power in sustained effort and dedication in the long haul to fewer tasks that we take on.

Brilliant ideas are found in the unfolding of thoughts. Our brains work better when we're not rushing. Doing fewer things means fewer mistakes, more creativity, and a higher quality of productivity. Remember, we are humans, not robots, and were made to go at a more natural pace. How often do you hear that in our rushed society?

By doing fewer things, you become a more authentic version of yourself

Doing less won't be easy at first. We have become accustomed to experiencing our life through others' opinions of going faster, multitasking, and taking on more.

The Art of the Calendar

Speaker and businessman Stephen Covey taught us about *big rocks* in the '90s, and it's a principal that holds the test of time. I remember going to one of his seminars, and they took out two big clear vases. In one, the instructor put a bunch of sand in the bottom, then he put in gravel then four big rocks which didn't fit. In the other he put in four big rocks; then he poured in the gravel and then packed in the sand. It all fit with room to spare. So, we must schedule our "big rocks." Today, it's sometimes-called *deep-work scheduling* or *time blocking*.

Most of us don't tactically organize our calendars; we have let our calendars run us for too long. It's time to take

---

[5] Tony Robbins' Tip for Finding Your Blueprint in Life | Fox Business

back what's rightfully ours because *our time is our life*. I have organized my calendar by day-task themes for deep work and core work, which are the things we do best and that bring the most results.

Time Blocking and the Overload Epidemic

Before you begin to formulate your time-block plan, you will need to come up with a simple workload management strategy. Most entrepreneurs have some type of team, even solopreneurs usually delegate something to a virtual assistant. You will need to create some type of document or board showing what is being worked on, who is working on each item, and what projects are waiting in the queue, helping you track all projects. This will give you a good overview of the logistics to reach your goals.

By time blocking, you will start to see the quality of your work increase, and with better quality work, your busywork will become less attractive.

A Look at the Hybrid Time-Block Calendar

On certain days, I schedule large blocks of time to work on themed goals, tasks, and projects. By blocking tasks by category and day, it lessens stops and starts to the flow of work, which is crucial to creativity and concentration.

Your smaller daily tasks or nonprofessional tasks can be placed around this blocked time ... and remember to leave white space for down time during the day.

Monday—Learning Day. I concentrate on the courses and certifications that I am working toward. My schedule is heavy with online courses, reading, taking notes, and research for my writing and speaking. I know I am not the only one who signs up for courses and doesn't get around to them.

Tuesday—Corporate Day. I work on all tactical things in my business. Is this the only day I work in my business? No, but this is the day that all business tasks take priority.

Wednesday—Creative Day. I concentrate on my coaching; published writing, blogs, and magazine articles; my podcast; putting signature talks together; and social media content.

Thursday—Appointments, Organizing, and Meeting Day.

I set up my physical appointments, lunches, doctors' appointments, and nonwork meetings; organize; and declutter my computer, photos, home, and office.

Friday—Personal Business Day. I concentrate on personal business, paying bills, personal finances, communications with my bookkeeper, and paying attention to my personal investments and real estate properties and investments.

The focused attention and sense of completion are heavenly, satisfying, and productive.

Each Woman's Life Comes with Different Seasons

Mompreneurs need to recognize life's seasonal distinctions and when it's time to give our superwoman cape a rest for a while, slow down, and take extra time with our children. When we are open to this, we take care of both our children's and our own needs. By being aware of the seasons of motherhood, we reduce our stress and striving.

For example, right now, as I mentioned, we are raising my 13-year-old grandson. I went through the seasons of child rearing from baby, small child, preteen, teenager, and young adult with my children at the same time I was creating and building my businesses. After my children were grown, my schedule was massively freed up. When tragedy struck our family, and I was awarded full custody of my grandson, I needed to switch my season and thoughts to that of the parent of a six-year-old child. When the pandemic hit, I had to switch again from being the parent of a six-year-old to homeschooling and reinventing my businesses to thrive in the pandemic.

This fall, he will step out of homeschooling and into eighth grade at a private school 40 minutes away from our home, and I will again step into a different season of motherhood, affording me more time in my business.

What made me so successful in parenting and running my businesses during this time was the awareness of my seasons and the self-adjustments that I made that brought me peace of mind instead of anxiety. Adjusting my mindset allowed me to quickly realize that I'm not going to get all my business and personal goals accomplished as quickly as in my older children's season or my empty nest season. From experience, I know this time with my grandson is for a season, and I can appreciate and enjoy the precious gifts I will receive during it, especially if I am not in an anxious state of mind. The gifts and the bond that have come from enjoying this time of raising my grandson are extraordinary, and the adjustments and planning have increased my business revenues by leaps and bounds.

I hope this has helped and know that I am here for you if you need support in your season. Please reach out to me.

About Theresa

Theresa Ream is the founder of several multimillion-dollar businesses known as the Ream Companies and has over 42 years of business success. She is known as the owner of the largest minority woman-owned restoration company on the central coast and beyond. The Ream Companies include Disaster Kleenup Specialists, FRSTeam, Flooring America's Floor Store USA, and Cypress Design & Build.

Theresa is also the founder of Feminine W.I.L.E.S lifestyle business consultants, and her passion is helping established CEOs and entrepreneurs. She utilizes her strong organizational, financial, marketing, and nurturing skills to help women eliminate overwhelm and get clarity in their businesses by coaching them in systems, marketing, and building happy teams. Theresa believes you must build the woman to build the business.

Theresa is also skilled in running multigenerational family-owned businesses. She's been honored as Best Woman-Owned Business on the Monterey Peninsula and Best Minority Owned Business of Monterey by Union Bank and KSBW News, along with being named The Woman of the Year by The Professional Women's Network of Monterey.

Theresa is a community leader; speaker; bestselling author; blogger; writer (as a business expert) for *Marketing, Media & Money Magazine*; podcast guest; and host of the Expert Insights podcast, as well as the current marketing director of the Professional Women's Network of Monterey and Professional Women's Network National.

When Theresa is not serving in her business and community, she is an avid reader and traveler, loves bootcamp-style workouts and riding her bike, and is happily raising and homeschooling her 13-year-old grandson, Cash, with her husband Terry.

Connect with Theresa

Instagram: Theresa_ream_ceo
Facebook: Theresa.ream.98
Email: Theresa@reamteam77.com

My Recipe for Lemonade

Kara Taylor

Have you ever felt like you were having an out-of-body experience, watching yourself from the outside looking in and thinking, *What am I doing with my life*? Or even, *Where did all these lemons come from?* Just a few years ago I found myself contemplating that exact question. I knew I was unhappy, but I felt stuck not knowing how I was going to crawl out of this dark hole.

Just a bit of a backstory … I joined the United States Air Force as a licensed clinical social worker in 2008. Sure, I had great and noble reasons to join the military but even more pressing for me was finding a job where I could excel in my career. I also did not have a love life at the time which made joining an easy decision for me. (Wouldn't you know that about three weeks after submitting my application, I met my now husband!) I used to get irritated when people would tell me that things happen when you least expect them, but I now have a much greater understanding of how the Law of Attraction works and how acceptance draws things toward you, not away from you.

The first few years of my career, I absolutely loved my job and was thriving! My husband and I married in 2011, and we spent four amazing years in Germany. The assignment was incredible. I worked with great people, and we traveled all over the UK and Europe. My favorite experience of all was giving birth to my son, Lincoln, while there. Although I was not thrilled about our next location stateside, I was excited to be back in the United States, closer to our families, and for the new leadership position I was given.

Although excited when I got to this assignment, I was met by the staff with a lot of cynicism. They were understaffed and clearly unhappy with their circumstances. It was a *work hard, play hard* base which meant that the mental health clinic I was now leading had to carry the weight of this mentality. I was initially optimistic that I would be able to make a difference, but that belief quickly dissipated after months and months of negativity.

Negativity bottled up inside eventually comes out in some way. For me, it started with my own mental health. I was incredibly stressed out, overwhelmed, and miserable in my professional life, which eventually spilled over into my personal life. My marriage was rocky, and the word *divorce* was thrown around. Meanwhile, something completely unexpected happened … I got pregnant! Although I was ecstatic to be pregnant (I always wanted two children), my husband and I were in a disgruntled marriage.

And then more lemons. Approximately 13 weeks into the pregnancy, I thought I was experiencing a menstrual cycle and assumed I had miscarried. I tearfully went to the emergency room but learned that I was still pregnant. I remember feeling shock and disbelief that this could be true because I had convinced myself otherwise. Of course, I was happy but also extremely confused. I immediately scheduled an appointment with an obstetrician and a few weeks later was diagnosed with placenta previa—a condition where my placenta was blocking my cervix. Right before my appointment, I had booked a trip to Disney World for our family to liven up our marriage (not going on vacations was a serious point of discontent between us). My doctor told me we could not go because I couldn't fly. I needed to be close to a hospital at all times as there was a good possibility I would bleed again and both of us could die if I did not get medical attention in time. It's a really weird mindset to be in when you are ecstatic to be pregnant yet terrified about what could lie ahead.

Fast forward a few weeks, Lincoln and I were watching cartoons one Saturday morning when I felt a gush of blood. I ran to the bathroom, panicking. All I heard in my head at that time was the doctor's voice warning me that we both could die. I remember yelling for Lincoln to get daddy. He was only three years old at the time, and it still breaks my heart to think of it. (I am tearing up as I write this even now.) My husband came running in from a deep sleep and called 911. As the ambulance rushed me off to the hospital, I'm pretty sure the EMT was also shaken up because I could feel his trembling hands applying pressure to stop the bleeding. Fortunately, the bleeding ceased, but I was given news that stopped me (and my family) in our tracks. I was going to be hospitalized for the duration of my pregnancy. I was 27 weeks pregnant at the time.

The plan was for me to have a C-section at 36 weeks, which meant nine weeks of hospitalization. Who wants to be hospitalized for nine weeks? No one! I had never been away from Lincoln that long, and quite honestly, that was the hardest part of it all. My husband really stepped up and took care of all our needs. He made sure Lincoln visited me every day, and snuggling with him was the highlight of my day!

So many people said to me, "I don't know if I could do what you are doing." I didn't have much of a choice, but I did have a choice in how I responded. You can sink or swim, and I decided to swim. I found ways to entertain myself: I went on Pinterest and learned how to make headbands and footwear for my daughter (I was carrying a girl), watched *a lot* of movies, took walks up and down the unit—which wasn't far but got me moving—and a lot of my friends and colleagues visited me from the base.

At 36 weeks, I delivered Roslyn via C-section as planned. The surgery went well considering the circumstances. I ended up losing over half of my blood, so we had to stay at the hospital a few extra days before leaving. Being off from work for nine weeks plus the 12 weeks of maternity leave was honestly just what I needed for my mental health. I came back to work feeling much more refreshed and upbeat. I also knew we would be moving again in just a few short months. In August 2018, we packed up our house yet again, and this time, moved our family from Kansas to Colorado. Surprisingly, the strain on our marriage lessened significantly with a change of scenery.

It's amazing what a change of scenery can do! Everything was great at my new job. I loved the staff I was leading, my commander, and the location! All was great ... until it wasn't. In March of 2020, at the onset of the pandemic, we lost two cadets to suicide within 48 hours of each other. I didn't know it at the time, but this would be a turning point in my career. It was the series of events from this moment on that ultimately led to my separation from the military. Working countless hours day in and day out with little to no respect or appreciation for what we, as mental health professionals, brought to the table burnt me out quickly.

You always hear people talk about defining moments in their lives; this was mine. It was a cold morning in January 2021. I signed into my computer only to find out that I had not been selected for a promotion. Rather than feel sorry for myself, I made the courageous decision to separate from the military after 13 years of service, not because I was upset about not being selected for the promotion, but because I knew that this was my opportunity to pursue my dream of coaching. I'm sure you have heard the saying, *When life throws you lemons, make lemonade*. That's exactly what I was going to do. As soon as I "hit the button" requesting separation, I felt a tremendous amount of relief and excitement rush over me.

The next few months are pretty much a blur. By July, we had moved back to Pennsylvania and by September, I was officially separated from active duty and a free woman! Words fall short to describe the amount of peace and happiness I felt after separating. I knew how incredibly stressed I felt before, but I hadn't realized just how much of a toll it had taken on me. I immediately transitioned into working for a private practice that specializes in treating obsessive-compulsive disorder and other anxiety disorders.

The plan was to build my coaching business while working at this private practice. Here's what really happened: I put hours into my business here and there, but I wasn't consistently working my business. It wasn't because I had lost my desire for coaching but because *all* the limiting beliefs started to surface, telling me I wasn't good enough and that I don't have what it takes to be a successful business owner. I let fear take the reins and played it "safe" by staying busy as a therapist for a good year before making the decision to consistently work my business.

I was introduced to world-renowned speaker and coach, Mary Morrissey, and The Brave Thinking Institute in October 2022. After attending her DreamBuilder LIVE virtual event, I made the bold decision to invest in their coaching program. I was excited and terrified, yet again, but knew this was my moment to change my life. A year later, I can proudly say I received my certification as both a DreamBuilder coach and life mastery consultant. Since becoming involved with The Brave Thinking Institute, I have more than quadrupled the number of clients I have been able to help; I started my own therapy business alongside my coaching business; and I have made some incredible health transformations along the way.

The tangible rewards of launching my own business are incredible, but the best part of this whole experience is the intangible reward of who I have become in the process. I am not the same stressed-out person who was miserable with her job and constantly doubting herself. For the first time in my life, I can truly say that I love myself and that I am enough. I am perfectly imperfect just as I am right now today!

I decided to share my story because I know there are other women and moms out there like me who doubt their abilities. Maybe you don't feel like you are enough or are terrified of putting yourself out there for fear of failure. If that resonates with you at all, I hope sharing what I have learned on my journey of transformation will help you navigate your own unique journey.

If you want to transform your life, it's essential that you have a clear blueprint or vision of what you want your dream life to be. The average person spends more time planning a vacation than they do a life they love living. Without a clearly defined vision, you will likely remain exactly where you are. Every day I recite my three-year vision of my dream life, saying it as if it's already happening. That alone is a huge power move because you are sending a signal to your subconscious that this is something you would love. Your subconscious mind does not understand the difference between the present and the future when you speak about the future as if it's already happening. I know many of us get caught up in the how, but it's not the *how* that will change our lives, it's the *what*!

To create transformation in your life, you need to set aside any old stories you have been holding onto and be willing to write a new story. We've all heard the common definition of insanity as *doing the same thing over and over again and expecting different results*. Recognize that the old story is not actually serving you, and, in fact, is keeping you stuck. You have the power right now to write the next chapter of your life exactly as you want it to be.

Lastly, do yourself a favor and invest in a coach who will help you identify all your limiting beliefs and fears. One who will push you when you need to be pushed, get you out of your comfort zone, help you face your fears like a boss, and ultimately live your dream life. I have invested in several different coaches and can tell you that with a great coach by your side, you can achieve incredible results in a short period of time. I know it can feel scary to face your biggest, and often unspoken fears, but I promise that once you do, you will find they are not actually as scary as you thought. Your dream is waiting for you to claim it …

go get it! The lemonade is always sweeter when you squeeze the lemons yourself!

About Kara

As a certified DreamBuilder Coach and Life Mastery Consultant with the Brave Thinking Institute: The Premiere Training Center for Transformational Coaching, Kara Taylor can help you create a life that you love living.

Kara specializes in helping heart-centered professionals build their dreams, accelerate their results and create richer, more fulfilling lives.

For over 20 years, Kara has been studying and implementing transformational success principles, and as a sought-after speaker, trainer, and certified coach, Kara's workshops and coaching programs help people break through limitations and achieve greater results than they've known before.

Kara's vast experience providing therapy and helping her clients make long-lasting behavioral changes as a licensed clinical social worker set her apart from other coaches.

In addition, having served in the United States Air Force for 14+ years, Kara Taylor's military training and experience have equipped her with exceptional leadership and communication skills and the ability to adapt quickly and persevere through any situation she encounters.

If you're looking to gain clarity and confidence and achieve your next level of success, while enjoying the highest levels of fulfillment in life, Kara's coaching programs can help you get there.

Connect with Kara

Want to discover your dream life?
Email Kara Taylor at kara@karataylorcoaching.com to learn more about how you can achieve your dreams and create a life you truly love living.
karataylorcoaching.com
Facebook: facebook.com/kara.taylor.355

Continuing the Connection

A Note from the Authors

Photo by Danielle Cubarney & MEDIA – The Creative Agency

It feels wrong to *end* a book about synergies. After all, the connections between motherhood and entrepreneurship don't end. You don't hang up your hat from being a mother and say, "my work here is done." Even if your days of comforting someone from a nightmare at three in the morning or cheering them on as they cross the finish line have wrapped up, you enter a new chapter, as some of the authors here have demonstrated.

And so it continues.

Like motherhood, the connections that the women of this book have formed among themselves and with you, the reader, will continue going strong, growing and changing as the seasons pass. The lessons we carry with us from the stories shared here will continue to impact every part of our lives, and yours, because you can't compartmentalize the pieces of your life. Your family and business lives often collide when you're a mother and entrepreneur. But we wouldn't want it any other way because of how powerful those lessons have made us when we switch back and forth.

Some of the authors were lucky enough to gather together for headshots and a couple group shots before this book was published, and many of us met in person for the first time that day. Yet, through this book, it felt like we all knew each other already. Even if our stories aren't the same, we share aspects of our stories, pieces of our hearts, with each other, and we are more alike than different from other sisters in the trenches. If you're going through a challenging time in motherhood, like so many of us do, we hope that our stories have helped bolster you through the storm.

If it feels aligned, please connect with the women of *Powerful Synergy* and check out our charity partner The Global Sisterhood. Their information is on the next page. Proceeds from this book benefit The Global Sisterhood nonprofit, and we hope to empower women worldwide through our stories!

About The Global Sisterhood

The Global Sisterhood 501(c)(3) educates while providing resources and networking for women and girls internationally. By forming connections and supporting each other's missions and movements, they provide sustainable ways for women throughout the world to make their goals and dreams a reality.

Since 2016, The Global Sisterhood has championed various uplifting efforts around the world, including founding a college for entrepreneurship in in Tanzania, #PopUpGiving in the Pittsburgh area providing various needs to women locally, and supporting the teaching of over 87,000 women in Nepal. Working side-by-side with their dozens of charity partnerships internationally, the Global Sisters have built an early childhood learning center, provided sustainable food and water sources, and taught and uplifted countless women and children in need. When asked what the Global Sisterhood does, Dr. Shellie Hipsky has been known to reply, "Whatever it takes!"

Founder and executive director Dr. Shellie Hipsky's accolades span from being recognized for her woman empowerment work on the covers of *Forbes*, *Elle*, and *Vogue*

Magazines to earning honors such as The Presidential Lifetime Achievement Award for Volunteer Service. She is dedicated to guiding women and girls toward their aspirations, underscoring her commitment to empowerment.

For more about The Global Sisterhood, including their monthly installments of *Inspiring Lives Magazine*, please visit https://www.globalsisterhoodonline.org/

About Cori Wamsley

Photo by Danielle Cubarney & MEDIA – The Creative Agency

Cori Wamsley, CEO of Aurora Corialis Publishing, works with leaders who have a transformational story to share. She helps them quickly and easily write and publish a book for their brand that helps them create a legacy and be seen as an expert while building a relationship with the reader. She also hosted the livestream podcast Page-Turner's Studio with Cori.

Cori has 20 years' experience as a professional writer and editor, including 10 years with the Departments of Energy and Justice and four years as the executive editor of *Inspiring Lives Magazine.*

Cori's book *Braving the Shore*, from the Soul Sisterhood Series, won first place in fiction at The Author Zone Awards in

2023, and Cori was a nominee for the Brave Women Project's Evolve Pillar Award the same year.

Cori has written nine fiction books and one nonfiction book, *The SPARK Method: How to Write a Book for Your Business Fast,* and contributed to two anthologies. Her eleventh book will be released in the spring of 2025.

For more information about Cori or Aurora Corialis Publishing, please visit www.auroracorialispublishing.com.

Milton Keynes UK
Ingram Content Group UK Ltd.
UKHW021424231024
450026UK00012BA/808